The Dutch world of painting

Exhibition and catalogue made possible by
the generous support of KLM Royal Dutch Airlines

# The Dutch world of painting
*Gary Schwartz*

Vancouver Art Gallery
April 6-June 29, 1986

An exhibition organized by the
Netherlands Office for Fine Arts

Copyright © 1986 by Gary Schwartz, The Vancouver Art Gallery
and the Rijksdienst Beeldende Kunst

Catalogue designed and produced by Staelenberg & Van de Griend,
Amsterdam

Editorial and production assistance by Gijs Wintgens

Printed by Drukkerij Nauta bv, Zutphen

Bound by Thieme bv, Zutphen

Produced in The Netherlands

Published by Uitgeverij Gary Schwartz, P.O. Box 162,
3600 AD Maarssen, The Netherlands

Distributed in North America by Abner Schram, Ltd.,
36 Park Street, Montclair, NJ 07042

Distributed in the United Kingdom by Trefoil Books, Limited,
13 St. John's Hill, London SW11

ISBN 90 6179 064 6

Contents

# Foreword

The Golden Age of Dutch Painting continues to fascinate historians and public alike. Hundreds of thousands of tourists each year visit the great museums of the Netherlands, such as the Rijksmuseum, the Mauritshuis, Museum Boymans-van Beuningen, the Frans Halsmuseum and the Amsterdam Historical Museum. Paintings by artists such as Rembrandt, Frans Hals, Vermeer, Ruysdael, Jan Steen, Nicolaes Maes, Emanuel de Witte and Vincent van Gogh, remain as compelling for the modern viewer as for their contemporary audiences.

In a rare opportunity, one hundred works by some of these great artists and others, from the collections of the great Dutch museums, will be exhibited at the Vancouver Art Gallery on the occasion of the city's centenary in 1986.

*The Dutch world of painting* is not a 'survey' exhibition presenting unrelated works. It is carefully selected, curated specifically for the Vancouver context, leading us through the fascinating corridors of Dutch society from the 1540s to the time of Vancouver's founding in the 1880s.

We explore the art world and its links to government as well as the world of trade and commerce. We learn that the outpouring of creative activity that marked Dutch society in the sixteenth and seventeenth centuries can be directly related to waves of immigration at that time.

Guest curator and art historian Gary Schwartz presents Dutch painting of this period, and its familiar masterworks, in a new and intriguing light. The worlds of government, religion, trade, learning and entertainment, were not merely visual sources for the painter. They gave the work its meaning and its market.

*The Dutch world of painting*, a special collaboration between the Netherlands Office for Fine Arts (Rijksdienst Beeldende Kunst) and the Vancouver Art Gallery, brings the history of Dutch culture vividly to life.

It is appropriate that this collaboration should take place on the occasion of Vancouver's Centenary. The British explorer, Captain Vancouver, after whom the city was named, was of Dutch descent, his ancestral home, Coevorden.

As in seventeenth-century Holland, the vitality of Vancouver's cultural life during the past hundred years can be traced to waves of immigration interacting with a powerful indigenous culture. Indeed, one of Vancouver's largest and most active immigrant communities is from the Netherlands.

During the research for this exhibition, we learnt that this is the second

centennial collaboration between Dutch museums and a Vancouver fine arts
institution. In 1958, on the centenary of the founding of British Columbia, the
Fine Arts Gallery at the University of British Columbia hosted *The changing
landscape of Holland* for the Vancouver International Festival. Ninety drawings
and watercolours were presented by artists such as Cuyp, van Gogh, van der
Heyden, Rembrandt and Ruysdael.

Nearly thirty years later the Vancouver Art Gallery was able to expand on
this project, further strengthening the cultural ties between Canada and the
Netherlands.

An exhibition of this complexity would not have been possible without
extraordinary effort, especially by the Director of the Netherlands Office for
Fine Arts, Robert de Haas, and his staff. We are indebted to them and to the
lenders to the exhibition for sharing with us *The Dutch world of painting*.

I would also like to acknowledge the contribution of His Worship, Mayor
Michael Harcourt, Chairman of the Vancouver Centennial Commission, who
has nurtured this exhibition since its inception; Mr. Bonar Lund, President of
the Board of Trustees of the Vancouver Art Gallery, who worked tirelessly to
ensure the exhibition became a reality, and Minister of Communications
Marcel Masse, for supporting the exhibition through the Government of
Canada's Insurance Program for Travelling Exhibitions.

Finally, I would like to express our particular appreciation to the sponsors of
this exhibition, KLM Royal Dutch Airlines, whose generous support has
ensured a Centennial Celebration worthy of the occasion.

Jo-Anne Birnie Danzker
Director
Vancouver Art Gallery

# Foreword

Children's birthdays can be important moments even in the lives of adults. The party, the presents, the treats can give a child an unforgettable radiant glow. But a birthday has its melancholy side as well, reminding parents how much older they are than their growing children.

This year the city of Vancouver turns one hundred. There are not more than a hardy handful in the old age homes of the Netherlands who can say the same. On the other hand, the average age of Dutch cities is between 700 and 750 years; and they will be forgiven if they smile a bit patronizingly at all the excitement in Vancouver.

The birthday present that Vancouver chose for itself – an exhibition covering three centuries of Dutch painting – is simple enough at first glance, an expression of the youthful boldness and justifiable ambition that characterize this important city and its splendid museum.

When I say that the exhibition is simple at first glance, I am thinking of the riches of the Dutch collections from which it is drawn. The English art historian Christopher Wright, in his publication *Paintings in Dutch museums*, listed some thirty thousand paintings by about three-and-a-half thousand masters in three hundred and fifty institutional collections. The total includes non-Dutch paintings, but far fewer than one might think. For all its international orientation, the Netherlands has never been seriously interested in collecting the art of other nations.

With such a vast number of paintings to choose from, it surely cannot have been difficult to treat Vancouver to an exhibition of a mere hundred works. A second glance, however, shows us how misleading this impression is. Organizing an exhibition of old art involves a lot more than taking a number of canvases from museum galleries and storerooms and loading them into a plane. It is a careful process of weighing the relative merits of all those works against each other, in search of the combination of artists and subjects which best illustrates the chosen theme. That is one of the differences between 1886 and 1986: the discipline of art history, which is not much older than the city of Vancouver, has not stood still in the intervening century.

At the risk of oversimplifying history, I think it can be said that a hundred years ago it dawned on us how few works by certain old Dutch masters were left in the Netherlands. Within the limits of the possible, we began to buy back Dutch paintings from abroad. At the same time, we began to comb the archives for accurate information concerning our old masters, who were only known from romanticized biographies. The researchers of the late nineteenth century set out to find facts that could help them to distinguish the work of one artist from that of another.

Guided by their aesthetic preferences, they devoted most of their attention initially to the great names: Frans Hals, Rembrandt van Rijn, Jacob van Ruisdael, Paulus Potter, Jan Steen. As research continued into our century, the names of many less familiar figures could be added to this honour roll, while the number of works assigned to the great masters was pared down by increasingly critical connoisseurs.

That is only one of the issues involved. Concurrently, twentieth-century scholars began to grow interested in other sides of art than the aesthetic one. They realized that the surrounding culture also affected the nature and style of a finished work. The implicit notion that a painting was a portrayal of reality – however you define it – began to lose ground. This insight had particularly far-reaching consequences for the study of Dutch art, which had always been seen as the most realistic school of all. Suddenly we were made aware of the moralizing, allegorical and symbolic meanings that could be concealed in a seemingly realistic representation.

Art history marches on. Gary Schwartz is a member of a new generation – not even such a young one, at that – which has brought yet other insights to bear on the same body of works. The present exhibition and catalogue are one of the first results of his approach, which he explains in the introduction. To assemble a survey of Dutch painting by the norms not of 1886 or 1936 but of 1986 was however only part of the challenge. We also wanted our bouquet to represent the entire artistic flora of Holland, while being harmonious and fragrant. I hope you will think we have succeeded.

It is my pleasant duty to express my thanks to Michael Francis, co-chairman of the Centennial Commission, and to my colleague Jo-Anne Birnie Danzker, director of the Vancouver Art Gallery, for their confidence in this venture. While it is true that they approached the Netherlands Office for Fine Arts rather late in the day for a project of this magnitude, they bore up well under the uncertainties they had to endure from our side.

Old art should be as fresh and new as contemporary art. If it stops surprising us, it ceases to be art. Should *The Dutch world of painting* live up to this criterion, we can say that the youthful centenarian Vancouver has chosen the right present.

Robert de Haas
Director
The Netherlands Office for Fine Arts

# Introduction

In 1981, my late teacher H. W. Janson, in a lecture at the university of
Groningen, took on a problem that had been nagging him for half a century:
does form really follow function, as the credo of the Modernist school has it? In
his student years the saying had the power of dogma, but Janson was never able
to come to grips with it in his own work on the art of sculpture. It may make
sense to analyze the form of works of applied art and architecture in terms of
function, but even then... Does function really dictate to the designer the
proportions, the surfaces of his creations? 'I wonder,' said Janson, 'whether it is
possible to find *any* kind of man-made object – tool, machine or work of art –
that has a purely functional shape.'[1]

Yet, one cannot simply throw the maxim overboard. For all its slogan-like
simplicity, it expresses an important thesis: that artistic form is not an
autonomous value, but is derived from other values. But if those values are not
primarily mechanical, as the early Modernists argued, what are they then? In his
lecture, which appeared in print after his death, Janson suggested that we
broaden the term 'function' to include not just the 'work' which a created
object is expected to perform, but also the 'task' faced by its maker, the artist.
Janson reminded his listeners that the great nineteenth-century cultural historian
Jakob Burckhardt, in his last years, challenged his followers to write a new
history of art, 'nach Aufgaben,' in terms of tasks. By way of example, Janson
demonstrated how a sculpture by Donatello could give expression to Florentine
civic patriotism, and a English tomb of the eighteenth century to prevailing
ideas about resurrection and immortality.

The message had a strong appeal to me. In my work on the history of Dutch
art of the seventeenth century I had been growing increasingly interested in the
way artists and their works functioned in society. I now began to examine this
aspect of the art world more systematically. What I noticed at once is that the
particular functions which had been studied by Burckhardt and Janson, and put
into practice by the Functionalists, were not applicable to Dutch painting. The
ideal Prince and his State, which obsessed Renaissance Italy, played but a small
role in Holland, where the source of political power was much more diffuse.
The philosophies of life and death debated so passionately in eighteenth-century
England were only beginning to be discussed by a few people in the
Netherlands of the previous century. Neither were the corporate images and
personal life styles which determine the function of much twentieth-century art

| FORM OF GOVERNMENT | YEAR | EVENT |
|---|---|---|
| Hereditary Hapsburg lands | 1555 | Philip II succeeds his father Charles V. Margaretha of Parma becomes governess of the Netherlands |
| | 1559 | Beginning of resistance to Hapsburg rule |
| Republic the United Netherlands | 1579 | The northern provinces sign the Union of Utrecht; begining of the Eighty Years War |
| | 1581 | The United Provinces abjure the rule of Philip II |
| | 1584 | Assassination of William the Silent, who as stadholder held the highest military post in the country and was regarded as the Father of his Country |
| | 1585 | William's son Maurits becomes stadholder |
| | 1609 | Twelve Years Truce with Spain; de facto recognition of the Republic |
| | 1618-1619 | Synod of Dordrecht; tensions between Remonstrants and Counter-Remonstrants stop just short of civil war |
| | 1625 | Death of Maurits; he is succeeded by his brother Frederik Hendrik, who successfully continues the war |
| | 1647 | Death of Frederik Hendrik; he is succeeded by his nineteen-year-old son Willem II |
| | 1648 | Treaty of Münster ends the Eighty Years War in favour of the Republic |
| | 1650 | Willem II launches abortive attack on Amsterdam; he dies later that year, and no new stadholder is named |
| | 1652-1654 | First Anglo-Dutch War |
| | 1665-1667 | Second Anglo-Dutch War |
| | 1672 | French invasion of Holland; son of Willem II |

|  |  | becomes stadholder as Willem III, who in 1689 becomes King William III of England |
|---|---|---|
|  | 1702 | After death of Willem III a second stadholderless period commences; in the War of the Spanish Succession the Republic fights with England against France |
|  | 1713 | Treaty of Utrecht ends war |
|  | 1747 | Willem IV, of the Frisian branch of the house of Orange, becomes stadholder |
|  | 1751 | Death of Willem IV; Third Stadholderless Period, which sees the rise of the anti-Orangist Patriots |
|  | 1780-1784 | Fourth Anglo-Dutch War, undermines international position of the Republic and weakens stadholder |
| Batavian Republic | 1795 | France invades, is supported by the Patriots; Willem V flees to England. |
|  | 1809 | Kingdom of Holland incorporated into France |
|  | 1813 | As Napoleonic Empire collapses, support for the House of Orange surfaces; son of Willem V returns to Holland and is proclaimed constitutional monarch |
| Kingdom of the Netherlands | 1814-1815 | Congress of Vienna joins the former Republic with the former Spanish Netherlands into a single kingdom under King Willem I |
|  | 1830-1831 | Southern Netherlanders rise in the successful Ten Days Campaign against the Dutch |
|  | 1839 | Definitive division of newly independent Belgium from Kingdom of the Netherlands |
|  | 1840 | Willem I resigns in favour of his son Willem II |
|  | 1848 | Constitution revised; powers of parliament enlarged, those of king reduced |
|  | 1849 | Willem II dies and is succeeded by Willem III |

relevant to the Dutch situation. It was in the social and religious spheres, in government and in foreign trade that Dutch art seemed to seek its subjects and from which it took its basic terms. Moreover, each of these spheres was coloured strongly by local interests. The English historian K.H.D. Haley describes this side of Dutch life tellingly: 'It was vital to know whether a Dutchman was an Amsterdammer or a Leidenaar or a Haarlemmer. If he was a townsman, he belonged to a fairly tightly-knit community, with its jealously guarded local customs, privileges and tradition, with its common concern for the maintenance of dykes and canals, its civic guards, its orphanages and almshouses, its council and its delegation voting as a body in the provincial States.'[2]

Even within a small community, however, there were antagonistic concerns as well as common ones. One has to know whether a Dutchman was a Calvinist or a Mennonite, a Remonstrant or a Catholic, to which of the rival patrician clans he belonged or adhered, and how well he stood with the members of his own and other groups.

In order to contribute anything of meaning to a culture of this kind, an artist had to be part of it. He or she had to operate – to function – from a position that was fixed in many ways, and linked by many routes to particular segments of society. Many works of art will have been seen by contemporaries not just as objects of beauty but as manifestations of particular meanings, attributes of a certain milieu. It became my aim to try to map those positions and routes, those meanings and milieus as accurately as possible. The existing literature on Dutch art was of little help in this regard. Art historians tend to be more interested in universal values than in local ones, and are all too quick to claim that the artists they admire transcend the here and the now. In studies on Jan van der Heyden and Rembrandt, I did my best to reconstruct the specific circumstances in which the artists lived, and to investigate the possible effects of the immediate environment on their art. [3]

When the invitation was extended to organize an exhibition for the Vancouver Art Gallery covering Dutch painting of three centuries, I accepted gladly, with the intention of testing my approach on a larger scale. Since only six months were available for choosing the works and writing the catalogue, and since the displays could only be drawn from The Netherlands Office for Fine Arts and the Dutch museums, it was clear from the start that the exhibition could not in any sense be a survey, let alone an exhaustive treatment, of the subject. The selection of paintings was guided by the desire to illustrate the social and political processes at work in the world of art. The paintings I was after were those which bore traces of their origin in a specific sector of society, and to demonstrate the artist's relation to it. It was not my expectation or intention that all the paintings in the show meet this criteria. That would give the viewer the impression that Dutch painting was nothing but a mirror of society, an impression I do not wish to create.

As research progressed, however, more and more of the exhibits took on closely defined historical contours. Even works which I initially thought of as counter-examples – paintings made for an impersonal market, out of purely commercial considerations – began to surprise me, and I began to wonder whether the localism and particularity of Dutch painting might be even more pervasive than I thought. One such painting is the town- and seascape by the highly commercial Haarlem specialist Hendrick Vroom. The work by him which I had chosen for the exhibition is a view of Delft (cat.nr. 81), a city with which he had no known connection. In writing the entry on the painting, I was pleasantly amazed to come across this document from the Delft archives pertaining to it: 'On June 23, 1634, Master Vroom of Haarlem presented the burgomasters of this city with a portrayal of Delft, painted by his own hand, in regard of the special affection he has always felt for this city, his mother being buried in the Old Church, and the aforesaid Master Vroom having learned his art here in his youth.' To paraphrase Janson: I wonder whether it is possible to find *any* Dutch painting – portrait, history or landscape – that has a purely artistic function.

Fortunately for the art historian and for the visitor to the exhibition, even this extreme possibility does not detract from the aesthetic value of the paintings. In choosing the works for the exhibition, I was able to indulge my taste for historical puzzle-solving and still come up with paintings that left me, at least momentarily, speechless with delight. I hope the exhibition will succeed in conveying both these pleasurable sensations to the visitor.

1. Janson 1982, p. 13.
2. Haley 1972, p. 195.
3. Schwartz 1983 and 1985.

**I**

ISAAC CLAESZ. VAN
SWANENBURGH
(1537–1614)
*Self-portrait.* Inscribed
'*AN°. DNI. 1568.*' Panel,
94 × 71.5 cm.

Leiden, Stedelijk Museum
De Lakenhal, inv.nr. 1738.
Purchased from the
Schaeffer Galleries, New
York, in 1974. Discovered
in 1965 in London by
Lodewijk Houthakker of
the Bernard Houthakker
gallery, Amsterdam.

The self-portrait of the
artist at his work was a
relatively new phenome-
non in 1568. Two years
earlier, van Swanenburgh's
kinsman and pupil Otto
van Veen painted himself
at the easel, in a room
filled with members
of his family.

Van Veen later moved
from Leiden to Antwerp
to become the teacher of
Peter Paul Rubens and a
famous man in his own
right. His painting has
been in the Louvre since
1835. In 1558, an image
closer in type to van
Swanenburgh's was
created by Anthonis Mor,
a portraitist from Utrecht
who in 1557 had painted
King Philip II of Spain and
was famous throughout
Europe. Mor's painting
hung in his house in
Utrecht in the 1560s, but
later entered the Medici
collection of self-portraits,
and is still in the Uffizi.

Swanenburgh's fame
remained limited to

Leiden, but in that little
pond he was undeniably a
big fish. In 1576 he had
been elected to the Leiden
town council, and in the
following four decades he
controlled all township
matters pertaining to art.
For all his talent and
influence, however, his
reputation did not carry
very far, and this painting,
one of his best, remained

unknown to art history
until its rediscovery
twenty years ago by the
distinguished Amsterdam
art dealer Lodewijk
Houthakker.

The painter's riveting
gaze draws our attention
irresistibly to his personal
appearance, but in the
corners of our eyes we see
the attributes that make
him what he is: the coat of

arms refer to his distin-
guished family back-
ground, the Renaissance
statuette and drawing sheet
to his solid artistic training,
and his hands, grasping
palette and brush, to his
innate talent.

Ekkart 1974, Ekkart 1978
and Ekkart 1979.

# The art world

For half the period covered by this exhibition, the Dutch world of painting searched for its identity abroad or in the past. Or both at once. 'I'm now properly French,' wrote the young Dutch painter Gerard Bilders in 1860 to his patron Johannes Kneppelhout, 'but in being properly French I am properly Dutch, since the great French artists of today have a lot in common with the great Dutch ones of the past'.[1] He was absolutely right. The Barbizon artists he so admired were in their turn worshippers of the Dutch seventeenth-century landscape painters.

Bilders's paradox shows us a Dutch art world unsure of where it stands: there was greatness in Dutch art, but where was it? The masterpieces of the golden age were the glory of Dresden, Paris and London. The inspiration that they gave off made the reputations of German painters of daily life, French painters of landscape and English portraitists. And who were the most successful Dutch painters of the nineteenth century? Ary Scheffer, a lion of Paris society, and Laurens Alma-Tadema of London. Even the unsuccessful Vincent van Gogh felt he had to go to France to find himself.

It was one of the times when the recurrent Dutch complaint hung heavy in the air: how can our tiny country, tucked away in a corner between Germany and France, with England on one side of our sea and Russia on the other, ever amount to anything in the world?

What made it all the more painful was that Bilders and his contemporaries were looking backwards across a period when there was so much promise in the air. After the Napoleonic Wars the Kingdom of the Netherlands had been called into being, a grand country comprising Holland and Belgium, under the son of the last Dutch stadholder, the first King of the Netherlands. He and his son, Willem I and Willem II, were interested in art; they patronized living artists, donated to campaigns to raise monuments to dead ones, and collected on their own; Willem II even designed and built a museum for his collection, the Gothic Hall in The Hague. However, the days of Great Netherlandish grandeur were numbered. The Belgians revolted in 1830, and in 1848 the prerogatives of the king were sharply curtailed. The leader of the Liberal Party, which now set the tone in political life, is quoted as having said: 'Art is no concern of the state's.' (In fact, the circumstances under which he said this make the statement less damning than it sounds, but it nonetheless became one of those quotations that give the outraged a battlecry.)

**2**

HERMAN VAN
VOLLENHOVEN (active
1611-1627 in Utrecht)
*Self-portrait painting old
couple.* Signed and dated
*H. Vollenhove An° 1612 in
Wtre....* Canvas, 89 × 112
cm.

Amsterdam, Rijks-
museum, inv.nr. A 889.
Purchased in 1873 from
the collection of D. van
der Kellen Jr. (1804-1879),
chief medallist of the State
Mint in Utrecht, where his
father worked as a
medallist before him.

The extremely strong
presence of the figures in
this intriguing painting,
combined with a nearly
total absence of informa-
tion concerning it and its
maker, leave the field
wide open to the observ-
er's fantasy. That of
professional art historians
has tended to concentrate
on the element of Vanitas:
the transience of all earthly
things, as expressed by the
skull and hourglass beside
the old couple. This fea-
ture of the painting is a
carryover from sixteenth-
century portraiture, where
the mortality of the sitters
is often underscored with
details of that kind.

How, however, are we
to interpret the portrait on
the easel? Is it too an
example of things that
pass, or is the painter's
work in oil supposed to
represent a triumph over
death (see the poem by Jan
Vos in chapter 2)?

Finally, what are we to
make of the position of the
painter? Van Swanen-
burgh's self-portrait
(cat.nr. 1) can be 'read' as
a painter at his easel
looking into a mirror and
depicting what he sees
there. If the reader tries
to figure out how van
Vollenhoven painted the
work before us, he will
end up in a conceptual
knot like those tied so
gladly by the twentieth-
century Dutch artist M.C.
Escher.

In the year of this
painting, van Vollenhoven
became a founding officer
of the Utrecht guild of
St.Luke. In 1626 he was
paid 700 guilders by the
States of Utrecht for a
painting they gave as a gift
to Amalia van Solms.

Kramm, vol.6, p.1787.
Würzbach, vol.2, p.810.

## 3

ARNOLD HOUBRAKEN
(1660-1719)
*A young artist painting a voluptuous nude model, an older friend looking over his shoulder.* Signed *A W Houbraken.* Panel, 28.5 × 19 cm.

Amsterdam, Rijksmuseum, inv. nr. C 153. On loan from the city of Amsterdam (A. van der Hoop bequest) since 1885.

Although the viewer is assumed to think no evil when admiring a painting of a nude, artists and their models are constantly aware of the erotic element in their relationship. Arnold Houbraken wrote about the phenomenon in his life of Rembrandt, in an anecdote which he probably embellished if he did not invent it. One of Rembrandt's pupils, he wrote, painting a nude model behind a partition on a hot summer day, got so warm that he too removed his clothing. His fellow students crept up on him and listened in on the double entendre being exchanged between the two. Rembrandt joined them, peeping at the couple through a crack in the wall, and when he heard the young man say: 'We're just like Adam and Eve in Paradise, being naked together like this,' he burst in on them saying 'Because you are naked, you have to leave Para-

dise,' and drove them into the street without letting them get dressed. (Rembrandt would seem to have shared Adriaan van Beverland's theory of original sin; see cat. nr. 74.)

In this painting, Houbraken shows a sensitivity to the joys of voyeurism. Seen through the eyes of the young painter, the model can be regarded as a studio aid; it is the appreciative gaze of the older man that turns her into a sex object. After registering that message, we notice the careless disarray of her shed garments, especially the slippers, which often serve in Dutch genre painting as an emblem of wantonness.

Exhib. cat. *Maler und Modell,* 1969, ad nr. 81.

19

**4**

JOHANNES JANSON
(1729-1784)
*Paulus van Spijk and his
wife Anna Louise van der
Meulen*. Panel, 76.5 × 56
cm.

Leiden, Stedelijk Museum
De Lakenhal, inv.nr. 3265.
Acquired in 1983 from
the collection of Miss
A.M.W. Weydung,
Leiden.

Paulus van Spijk (1727-
1779) was a Leiden brewer
and dilletante, a member
of the local society Art is
Acquired through Labour
(see under nr. 80). The art
historian A. Staring was
able to identify him and
his wife as the sitters of this
portrait through the work
on the easel, which corresponds to a catalogue entry
in the auction of van
Spijk's art collection in
1781: 'A dune landscape,...
with an ox grazing on a
hillock, in addition to
several sheep and a seated
man; in the foreground is a
red ox and drinking billy-
goat. Very warm in
tone...'

It stands to reason that
the painter of the land-
scape, Johannes Janson,
was also the author of the
double portrait, which is
unsigned. In fact, the van
Spijks were patrons of
Janson, owning at least 24
paintings by him. Twenty-
three were in the auction,
but this painting – Janson's
only known portrait – was
apparently kept in the

family. The owner from
which it was acquired in
1983, Miss Weydung, is
the descendant of a sister
of the childless van Spijk.

Staring 1953. Pelinck 1953.

and

**5**
*Hilly landscape with cattle,
sheep and a herdsman*. Panel,
63 × 54 cm.

Leiden, Stedelijk Museum

De Lakenhal, cat.nr. 225.
Presented to the museum
in 1893 by Dr. W.N.du
Rieu, who also donated
to the Lakenhal three other
paintings by Janson and a
fourth he thought was by
the same master, along
with four other paintings.

A landscape much like the
unframed work on the
easel in Janson's painting
of the van Spijks (see nr. 4).
The artist sometimes
produced such paintings

on commission, as when
he made a landscape of a
certain type and format to
match one by his colleague
Franciscus Xavery in the
van Spijk collection. The
easy acceptance by his
patrons of Janson's work is
typical of the undemand-
ingness of the Leiden art
world in the later eight-
eenth century.

See also nr. 80.

**6**

WILLEM BARTEL VAN
DER KOOI (1768-1836)
*The drawing lesson of Anna
Charlotte Didier de Boncour
(1748-1802).* Signed and
dated *W.B. v.d. Kooi/inv.
et fec.1793.* Canvas,
42.5 × 52 cm.

Leeuwarden, Fries
Museum, inv.nr. 1969-46.
Purchased at sale Luzern,
28 November 1967, lot
2281.

The woman at the table
was identified by C.
Boschma, director of the
Fries Museum, as the fifty-
one-year-old amateur
artist Anna Charlotte
Didier de Boncour. Anna
Charlotte studied drawing
in The Hague, where she
was born, under Dirk
Kuipers. She left there for
Leeuwarden in 1775 when
she married the three-year
younger Henricus van der
Haer, registrar of the
Court of Friesland. In that
provincial capital she made

the acquaintance of van
der Kooi, who wrote in
later years that he 'had the
honour of being acquaint-
ed with her house-hold
several years before her
death.' He said this in a
letter to the art historian
Adriaan van der Willigen,
advising him to include
the artist in his forth-
coming history of Dutch
painting. (Anna Char-
lotte's name is not to be
found in the four-volume
work.)

There can be little doubt

that the standing man
behind the draughts-
woman is van der Kooi at
the age of forty-five;
Boschma's identifications
of the other figures as
members of Anna Char-
lotte's family are very
plausible.

Van der Kooi came
from a family of Friesland
civil servants. He was a
committed patriot, and
under the Batavian
Republic served as a
representative in the
provincial assembly. In

Preceding the Kingdom of the Netherlands, there were no Netherlands at all, for a brief period. Napoleon had incorporated the Dutch state into France, as eight distant northern *départements*. The French influence on the art life of the country was far-reaching in the extreme. On the positive side we can count the institution of an Academy for art education, which proved to be a major permanent contribution. But for as long as Napoleon ruled Europe (and his brother Louis Napoleon ruled Holland), the negative aspect of being a French province was far more apparent: the French simply carted off to Paris the major art treasures of the Netherlands. It took a lot of doing at and after the Council of Vienna to get them back. In fact, the most recent catalogues of collections like the Royal Picture Gallery and the National Print Room still contain lists of objects which were never retrieved from France after 1815.

To a latter nineteenth-century Dutch art lover looking backwards across these periods of unreal imperial pretension, the eighteenth century must have looked pretty much like a blank. How could it have been otherwise, if he found his eighteenth-century counterparts also looking over their shoulders at the past? The artists took the terms of their creativity from their forebears of a century before, and the collectors, agreeing with them, bought old art first and new art last.

The only museum in the country was the collection of the last stadholder of the Republic, Willem v. In 1773 he bought a building across the street from the seat of the government, refurbished the upper story as one long gallery, filled it from floor to ceiling with paintings and opened it to the public. There were a few burghers with collections that rivalled the stadholder's, and who installed them in cabinets where they held private salons.

It was in these same circles – the court at The Hague and a handful of art-loving patricians in the large cities – that living artists would find their patrons. The sharp distinction between collectors of modern art and old masters which is characteristic of the twentieth century had not yet come into being.

1798 he was appointed Lecturer of Drawing at the Frisian university of Franeker (where young Bonifacius van der Haer, whom we see from the back in this painting, began his law studies the year before).

Boschma 1978.

Interestingly, despite French cultural supremacy, the collectors of Holland bought nearly only works by Dutch artists. In the stadholder's gallery there were 130 paintings by Dutch masters as against five by Frenchmen.[2] The foreign paintings that were collected here in the eighteenth century were almost all sold abroad afterwards. The Amsterdam merchant Gerrit Braamcamp, for instance, owned 33 paintings by French and Italian artists; none of them, as far as we know, is still in Holland. For that matter, even of his 235 Dutch paintings, today only thirteen are in Dutch museums, as compared to seven in the Louvre, to name only the largest of the foreign heirs to the collection.[3]

The strongest feature of the Dutch art world in the eighteenth century, as these figures reveal, was trading and exporting art. The town of Amsterdam

**7**

HENDRIK JAN VAN
AMEROM (1777–1833)
*Self-portrait with wife and
son.* Signed and dated *H. J.
v. Amerom fec. 1804.*
Canvas, 56.5 × 42 cm.

Arnhem, Gemeente-
museum, inv. nr. GM 2007.
Presented by C. 't Hooft,
director of the Fodor
Museum, Amsterdam, in
1929.

The painter drinks a cup of
tea poured by his homely
wife while they gaze at
each other soulfully. It is
their son who establishes
eye contact with the
observer – from behind a
parapet, holding on to his
mother's skirt for added
safety.

While the same tools
and signs of the artist's
trade are displayed by the
shy van Amerom as by the

ran auctions, through the orphans' court, which were to become the model for art sales throughout Europe. And the strongest part of the market in those auctions, by far, was the sale to foreign dealers of seventeenth-century Dutch paintings, for steadily rising prices.

Among all the uncertainties and shifts of taste and judgment in the history of art, one of the great constants has been the popularity of Dutch painting of the seventeenth century. The praise of the Golden Age and the high worth put on its best products weighed heavily on Dutch artists of later periods. If they themselves were not measuring the value of their work against that of Rembrandt, Jan Steen and Jacob van Ruysdael, others were. And the later generations seldom came out well in the comparison. Whereas in the 1600s collectors were willing to pay as much for a new painting as for an old one, in the following century, a small sample reveals, contemporary work had dropped to about two-thirds the price of old art.[4]

The seventeenth century saw the rise of the specialties which still represent old Dutch art to many people: still-life, landscape, townscape, genre painting, church painting and so forth. In the course of the century, the new specialties gained ground at the expense of biblical and historical subjects, while the older specialty of portraiture held a fairly constant share of painterly production.

The vigour of the art scene in the seventeenth century did not assure painters of a good income. Fierce competition, chronic overproduction and the instability of the market caused serious financial difficulties. As a result of these factors, and the easy appeal of so much Dutch art, thousands of Dutch paintings went across the borders, and hundreds of painters as well, many of them permanently.

In the sixteenth century, the opposite situation prevailed. The 1570s and '80s saw the influx into Holland of hundreds of immigrant artists from the southern Netherlands, among the tens of thousands of Flemish Protestants seeking refuge from Spanish oppression. It was this massive injection of talent that gave the Dutch world of painting the volume and quality it needed to take over the leading position in northern European art that had been held in earlier centuries by Antwerp, Bruges and Ghent. Those centres were large-scale exporters of art, and their foreign contacts were now available to the Dutch. This helped to establish the world-wide reputation that Dutch art still enjoys.

The immigrant artists even brought part of their home market with them – entire tribes of cultured Flemings who settled in the same cities of the north as did the artists. In some basic respects, then, the art world that was the lasting pride of the Dutch Golden Age was actually Flemish. It was the misfortune of Flanders that its Spanish masters drove out some of the most talented people in the country, just as, under different circumstances, they expelled the Jews from

energetic van Swanenburgh (cat.nr. 1), there is a world of difference between what the two men do with them. Van Swanenburgh deploys them to demonstrate his social and professional status while van Amerom, who taught drawing at at the Arnhem academy, lounges among them, as if he were the attribute, a slave to art and family love. Yet he is not being quite as candid with us as he makes himself out to be. A contemporary biographer tells us that van Amerom was lame in one leg from an accident, and that he walked on crutches. In the painting, he disguises his handicap as romantic nonchalance.

Van Eijnden and van der Willigen, vol.3, pp.212-213. Immerzeel 1842, p.7.

**8**

AUGUSTUS ALLEBÉ (1838–1927)
*The museum guard*. Signed and dated *Allebé Bruxelles 1870*. Panel, 61.7 × 33.7 cm.

The Hague, Mesdag Museum, inv.nr. 2. Probably acquired by H. W. Mesdag at a lottery for victims of the Boer War.

and

**9**

*The exhibition*. Signed and dated *Allebé 1870*. 61.7 × 52 cm.

Amsterdam, Stedelijk Museum, inv.nr. A 2173. Presented to the museum by a relative of the art dealer C.M. van Gogh.

Nrs. 8 and 9 were originally parts of a single painting which the artist himself dismembered and gave away to two different parties: *The guard* to a charity sale and *The exhibition* to a relative of the art dealer C.M. van Gogh. Elie van Schendel, in the catalogue of the Mesdag Museum, suggests an intriguing reason for this act of artistic desperation: 'Allebé was in Brussels from 1868 to 1870. In the latter year his brief career

as a painter virtually came to a close, with his appointment as professor at the State Academy for Fine Arts in Amsterdam. This left him very little time for his own work, especially after he became director in 1880. His diaries and correspondence... reveal that he was moreover extremely insecure about his work and was afraid, as a professor, of being criticized for showing such old-fashioned, romantic paintings. This may have had something to do with the dismemberment of the painting.'
  A sad case, especially

since, as van Schendel also reports, the artist was especially fond of the painting. He copied *The guard* on a smaller scale to be presented to King Willem III on his silver anniversary in 1874, under the title 'Soliloquoy,' and seems to have named the large version 'An old friend.'

Van Schendel 1975, nr. 2.

their own country a century earlier. The Flemish influence in Holland, which is only beginning to be understood, helped give Holland the cultural radiance of the Golden Age.

A hundred years later the Netherlands received a new wave of immigrants from the south – French Huguenots who moved to Holland in 1685 after the revocation of the Edict of Nantes. With the memory still alive of the great boon of Flemish immigration in the 1580s, many Dutch cities opened their doors wide to the French Protestants. However, the wonder was not repeated. Most Huguenots who were active in the arts continued to think of themselves as Frenchmen, regarding their Dutch basis as an exile. Whatever fresh cultural stimuli they experienced benefitted France in the first place, through the immense intellectual traffic that developed between the Huguenots in Holland and their contacts in the home country.

Throughout the rest of our period, Holland was left unshaken by any great demographic shifts. It could be argued that this robbed the culture of elan, and led it to look across the border and into the past for clues to its own value.

1. Bilders 1974, p.70.
2. Brenninkmeyer- de Rooij 1977.
3. Bille 1961.
4. These figures are based on a comparison of the prices paid for works from the Braamcamp collection in 1771 (Bille 1961) and the valuations put on the stock of the major Amsterdam art dealer Johannes de Renialme upon his death in 1657 (Bredius 1915-1921, vol. 1, pp.230-239).

Fig. 1

REMBRANDT VAN RIJN
*Portrait of a man.* Signed
and dated *Rembrandt. f.
1650*. Canvas, 79.5 × 66
cm. The Hague, Maurits-
huis.

# Government

The two earliest artists represented in this exhibition are Adriaen van Cronenburgh, who was active between 1552 and 1590, and Isaac Claesz. van Swanenburgh, who was born in 1537 and died in 1614. Both men were not only painters but also government officials. Van Cronenburgh was the secretary of a district in Friesland called Tietjerksteradeel, and van Swanenburgh was councilman and burgomaster of Leiden. A number of his sons were city officials, some were artists, and at least one was both. Van Cronenburgh painted portraits of the Frisian nobility, who were still the local

Fig.2
ISAAC CLAESZ. VAN SWANENBURGH
*The spinning, reeling, warping and weaving of wool,* 1602. Panel, 137.5 × 196 cm. Leiden, Stedelijk Museum De Lakenhal.

rulers in his time, and van Swanenburgh designed stained glass for public buildings in Leiden and worked for township bodies such as the drapers' guild (fig.2).

The combination of professions was not unusual in the sixteenth and seventeenth centuries. In all parts of the country, at all levels of government, one comes across painters in office. Some of the better known examples are Aelbert Cuyp, who was a member of the High Court of South Holland for three years, and Gerard Terborch, who was on the town council of Zwolle.[1] Many more came from patrician families or married into them.

It would be a mistake to think that the public offices held by these artists were bestowed on them in recognition of their creative gifts. In general, political office in the Netherlands was reserved for the members of patrician families. Not even success in trade was enough in itself. The richest merchants of seventeenth-century Amsterdam, the Trips, were kept out of public office for half a century after moving to the city, until they managed to marry into one of the right Amsterdam families. No, we must assume that the artists gained their posts as a result firstly of family connections, secondly of social status, and thirdly of political ability (or submissiveness).

Most of the painters with government positions worked for their political masters or institutions over which they exercised control. Nowadays, an artist serving even on an advisory committee, let alone a legislative body, would be disqualified for such commissions. Were any sixteenth- or seventeenth-century eyebrows raised by these conflicts of interest? It is hard to say. No indignant outcries against artist-politicians who gave themselves commissions paid for out of tax money have been recorded. We might observe, however, that public offices held by painters did not become part of their artistic biographies. The first Dutch book of artists' lives – *Het schilder-boeck*, the Painter's book, by Carel van Mander – was written around the turn of the seventeenth century. In it, the author described and glorified the careers of the painters of antiquity, of Renaissance Italy and of northern Europe in the fifteenth and sixteenth centuries. Although van Mander was a writer who was quick to exaggerate the successes of his colleagues, he shows a notable disinterest in the political careers of artists, even going so far as to omit from his book altogether the artists who reached the highest stations in non-artistic life. His close contemporary, the Leiden burgomaster van Swanenburgh, for example, is mentioned only in the appendix, as the teacher of Otto van Veen. The omission was noticed with wonderment by van Mander's eighteenth-century successor Arnold Houbraken, and by others since. The question is of a kind that cannot be answered satisfactorily: 'Why did Carel van Mander *not* describe the career of this or that particular artist?' The answer I used to prefer, in the case of van Swanenburgh, was: 'Because van Mander felt that Isaac Claesz. used his political influence in Leiden to benefit only himself and his family, and crowded out van Mander and the rest of his colleagues.' But that explanation does not account for van Mander's omission of *all* mention of the political dimension in painters' lives. When he writes of Pieter van Veen, well on his way to political prominence in The Hague and Leiden, all van Mander said of him was that he was an astonishingly good painter, and that all agreed it was a pity he did not turn to art full-time. I find myself, therefore, tending towards some new kind of explanation, such as: 'Van Mander did not wish to draw attention to the kind of artistic successes attained by means of family ties or

**10**

ADRIAEN VAN
CRONENBURG (active
1547-90)
*Rienk van Cammingha
(d. 1598)*. Dated 1552.
Panel, 91 × 78 cm.

Leeuwarden, Fries Museum, inv.nr. 1887. On loan since 1881 from the van Cammingha family, who presented it to the museum in 1977.

Van Cronenburg, a native of West Friesland, across the Zuider Zee, was one of earliest artists to work in Friesland. His identity was established by the former director of the Fries Museum, A. Wassenbergh, on the basis of his signature, *A.a.a.a. van Cronenburg.* For many years, the illogical signature was 'corrected' to 'Anna van Cronenburg,' but Wassenbergh showed that the four a's were a rebus for Adriaen. In Dutch *A.a.a.a.*, read as 'A, three a's,' is pronounced 'A, drie a'en,' or Adriaen. The painter's cousin Jacob van Cronenburg had moved to Friesland before him, as a physician, and had married into not one but two families of local aristocrats, in two marriages. It was probably thanks to his connections that Adriaen was appointed secretary of Tietjerksteradeel in 1567. In 1580 he was forced to leave the province on account of his refusal to give up Catholicism and abjure Philip II. By 1584 he had returned.

The castle in the background is Camminghamburg, the family seat of the sitter, which was demolished in 1811.

Museum information.

**II**

CORNELIS CORNELISZ.
VAN HAARLEM (1562-
1638)
*A monk squeezing the breast
of a nun*. Painted in or
shortly before 1591.
Canvas, 116 × 103 cm.

Haarlem, Frans Hals-
museum, inv.nr.I-50.

From the Prinsenhof, for
which it was purchased in
1591 by the township of
Haarlem from the artist.

For two alternative
interpretations of the
painting – one as an attack
on monastic morals, the
other as a miraculous
proof of the triumph of

true faith – see the text.
The earliest known inter-
pretation, in a mid-eight-
eenth-century description
of the paintings in the
Haarlem town hall and
Prinsenhof, sees it as a
satire. In the context of the
commission – the painting
was ordered for a building
that had shortly before

been confiscated from the
Catholic church – this
seems the most likely ex-
planation. However, the
expressions of the two
figures seem to this viewer
more pious than prurient.

Biesboer 1983, p. 28

political influence.' He was a pedagogue, and preferred to project a picture of young artists discovering their talent and developing it by keeping their noses to the grindstone. When they are rewarded with prestigious commissions, it should be for their artistic attainments, not for their connections.

That is not the same thing as saying that an artist should not seek the favour of the powers that be. On the contrary – if van Mander's book has a message, it is that the arts need the support of rulers, governments, holders of high office and wealthy individuals. 'If the art of painting lacked such noble admirers, that art and its skilled practitioners would be reckoned among the gross handicrafts and handcraftsmen respectively, relegated in dishonour and contempt to the ignorant, uncomprehending commoners.' The great social and economic aim of the artist was to rise above that level once and for all. And the way to achieve it was to have one's patrons not among 'uncomprehending commoners' but among 'noble admirers' of painting.

One form of patronage which could be solicited rather easily was the commissioning of portraits. By the sixteenth century, the wealthier Dutch burghers as well as the nobility were in the habit of hanging family portraits on the walls. This continued throughout the seventeenth and eighteenth centuries; in this period about one in five of the paintings in Dutch homes was a portrait. There were also increasing numbers of miniature portraits being made and worn.

In an age such as our own, when many people have photographic portraits of themselves and their family on mantlepieces, desktops and in their wallets, this phenomenon does not seem to require special explanation. A more specifically Dutch tradition was the painting of group portraits of the members of certain civic bodies. We all have such pictures engraved in our mind's eye, thanks to the fame of the examples painted by Rembrandt and Frans Hals. Rembrandt painted four group portraits, of Amsterdam burghers: two of members of the surgeons' guild, attending anatomy lectures; one of a civic guard company, the *Nightwatch*; and one of the sampling officials of the drapers' guild. Hals painted nine: one Amsterdam civic guard company (actually, he only painted half of it – it was finished by the Amsterdam artist Pieter Codde); five Haarlem companies; and three of the governors and governesses of a home for the aged and a hospital in Haarlem.

However, none of these depicted ruling bodies. In fact, very few Dutch group portraits do. Most of them are of civic-guard companies (in the sixteenth and seventeenth centuries), guild boards (sixteenth and seventeenth) and the governors of charitable, medical and penal institutions (sixteenth to eighteenth centuries). The members of these bodies came from good families, but most of them never rose higher in the political hierarchy than the position in which we see them in the painted group.

**12**

THOMAS DE KEYSER
(1596–1667)
*Portrait sketch of Burgo-
master Abraham Boom,
Cornelisz.* Panel,
23.5 × 17.5 cm.

The Netherlands Office
for Fine Arts, inv.nr.NK
1420 (on loan to Amster-
dams Historisch Museum,
Amsterdam). Confiscated
by the Germans from the
collection of H.L. Larsen,
Wassenaar.

Said to be related to de
Keyser's unusual painting
of the four burgomasters
of Amsterdam being
informed of the arrival
of Maria de' Medici in
September 1638. That
visit was the occasion of
mammoth public cere-
monies which turned the
entire city into one big
stage starring the mother
of the king of France (with
whom she was having a
royal feud). Meeting the
queen-mother at the city
gates was Andries Bicker,
the most powerful man
in the city, while the
burgomasters who ruled at
his discretion stayed in
their chamber. Although
Thomas de Keyser was
well connected in Am-
sterdam officialdom, his
father having been town
architect and sculptor until
his death in 1621, he does
not seem to have been one
of the artists whose talents
were employed to lend
splendour to the occasion.
The painting of the four

burgomasters is quite small
and informal, and was
apparently intended as the
model for a larger version
which was not commis-
sioned. The composition
was published as a print
by Jonas Suyderhoef.

Cat. Mauritshuis 1977,
p. 132

**13**

BARTHOLOMEUS VAN
DER HELST (1613-1670)
*Four governors of the
Musketeers practice range,
Amsterdam.* Signed and
dated *Bartholomeus.vander.
Helst 1655.* Canvas,
171 × 283 cm.

Amsterdam, Amsterdams
Historisch Museum,
inv.nr. 171 (A 2010). From
the Musketeers practice
range (Kloveniersdoelen).

The civic guard of Am-
sterdam was far more
important as a political
institution than a military
one. The only time it was
called to arms during the
tenure of the gentlemen in
this portrait was during an
operetta battle in 1650,
when the 24-year-old

Stadholder Willem II tried
to take the city by surprise.

The gentlemen at the
table are, from left to
right: Cornelis Witsen
(1605-1669), a political
heavyweight who served
the first of his four terms
as burgomaster in 1653;
Roelof Bicker (1611-
1656), cousin of Andries
Bicker, who was the
uncrowned king of the
city until he was deposed
in the wake of the 1650
fiasco; Simon van Hoorn
(1618-1667), alderman
and future burgomaster;
and Gerrit Reynst (1599-
1658), alderman, the
richest of the four and one
of the most important
Dutch art collectors of his
time. All were members of
the town council, which
they entered in short

succession of each other in
the 1640s.

The practice ranges of
Amsterdam echoed less
often with the roar of the
musket and the swish of
the arrow than with the
clink of the mug. On off
hours, the premises were
run as taverns by con-
cessionaires. The licensee
of the Musketeers range,
whom we see behind the
figures at the table, was the
painter's brother. Not that
van der Helst needed such
connections for the com-
mission. He was the
leading group portraitist of
the city in these years, and
painted the governors of
the other practice ranges –
that of the handbow and
footbow guards – in 1653
and 1656 respectively. In
life as in art, he cultivated

a hard-edged style that
appealed to the he-men of
town hall.

Cat. Amsterdams
Historisch Museum 1975/
1979. De Gelder 1921.

**14**

GOVERT FLINCK (1615-1660)

*Gerard Pietersz. Hulft (1621-1656).* Signed and dated *G. Flinck f. 1654.* Inscribed *Nil adeo fuit unquam tam dispar sibi* (Nothing has ever been more unlike itself). Canvas, 130 × 103 cm.

Amsterdam, Rijksmuseum, inv.nr. A 3103. Bequeathed by Baroness Taets van Amerongen, 1930.

The oval portrait of Hulft is propped up on an overloaded desk filled with mementoes of the sitter's interesting life. The bound volumes and loose documents on the upper shelf refer to his tenure as town secretary of Amsterdam from 1645 until 1653, the charts and navigational instruments below to his career at sea. After the seizure by the British in 1652 of a merchant fleet in which he had invested a fortune, he hired twenty-four sailors to fight under him in the fleet of Admiral Witte de Witt. An ambivalent gesture, combining material support with a vote of no confidence. In the painting, the transformation from bookworm to man of action is symbolized by the drawing in the lower center, depicting a caterpillar on a leaf and a butterfly.

The loss of so much money was not Hulft's only problem. In 1653 he also lost his job as town secretary following a conflict with the burgomasters. They requested him to change the wording of a resolution that had been taken by the council, which he refused to do. Again, he took to sea, this time for the Dutch East Indies, with an appointment as director-general in his pouch. However, he was unable to get on with the governor-general, who sent him on a dangerous mission to Ceylon, where he was killed.

Hulft seems to have been the friend and protector of the painter, Govert Flinck, and of the poet Joost van den Vondel as well. Hulft was a member of the Remonstrant church, whose adherents were ejected from all government positions in 1619. Nonetheless, they retained considerable influence, especially in Amsterdam, and were able to re-enter the government there in later years. Flinck became a Remonstrant in 1651, leaving the Mennonite church in which he was born. Vondel too was a non-Calvinist – born Mennonite, he converted to Catholicism in 1640.

Vondel wrote a poem on Flinck's painting, and another on the engraving after the central section, the portrait. The phrase he found to describe Hulft's troubles with the burgomasters was: 'The town hall was too small for such a valiant man.' When the news reached Amsterdam that Hulft had been wounded, Vondel prepared to send him his own portrait, also painted by Flinck, with a poem saying that he dreamt of Hulft being hurt while hunting doves. Before he could get the painting onto an outgoing ship, the report was received of Hulft's death at Colombo. Vondel now interpreted his dream as an omen, 'for Colombo, where the good man died, means dove.'

The poems that Vondel wrote on Flinck's portrait of himself and of Hulft were the first of about twenty that he wrote on the painter and his works, between 1653 and 1660, when Flinck died. This all took place in the period when the new town hall was being decorated, for a large part with paintings by Flinck, based on ideas supplied by Vondel. The burgomasters who were in charge of the project, Cornelis de Graeff and Joan Huydecoper, were also the protectors of Hulft, the ones who recommended him for his position in the Indies. I would interpret all of this to mean that Hulft was helping Flinck and Vondel to get commissions for the town hall decorations. A painting such as this, glorifying a sitter, would be a normal way for a seventeenth-century painter to thank a patron for his help. The unusually rich program for the portrait is the kind of thing that Vondel would have thought up.

For Hulft, see de Balbian Verster 1932 and Rauws 1936-37.

When it came to official portraiture, the aristocracy remained better customers than burgher functionaries. We are used to thinking of the old Dutch state as a burgher republic, but in the longer line of history, the Republic was a passing episode of just over two hundred years, sandwiched between centuries of rule by feudal masters and modern royalty. And even in the intervening period, the Dutch nobility fared better as a class than is generally thought. In some provinces, it was even still represented in government as an estate. What is perhaps more to the point is that successful families of burgher patricians began early on to aspire to the condition of nobility. They would buy or marry titles, sometimes adopting embarrassingly transparent historical fictions to lend credence to their claims of ancient lineage.

And of course there was always the House of Orange, which, even as office-holders in a Republic, was royal enough for the stadholders and their consorts to be painted in hundreds of state portraits. Some of these images were entrusted to true court portraitists, such as the Swiss-born Benjamin Samuel Bolomey, who worked for Stadholder Willem v.

Most portraitists, however, enjoyed no special status, let alone paid positions at court. They competed with each other, in price, quality and connections, for invitations to paint members of the House of Orange. It was worth some effort to become a painter to the stadholder or king. A portrait commission could be followed by the purchase of other work. Rembrandt, for example, painted the wife of Stadholder Frederik Hendrik in 1632, during a period when he also sold some twelve other paintings to the court, for excellent prices.

The reputation of being a court painter also helped an artist sell his work to the lower nobility and bourgeoisie, like any other 'purveyor to His Majesty.' The glow emanating from the throne or the burgomaster's seat (in Dutch one speaks of the 'cushion') would reflect on artists who painted the dignitaries who sat on them.

There is a fascinating difference between the two groups: the painters who had political positions of their own, and those who were dependent on the favour of the great. The first kind enjoyed a status in society which was higher than that of a mere painter; their work as artists could only lower them in the eyes of their contemporaries, not raise them. In fact, many of them stopped painting once they had achieved high office.

Those who lacked independent status, however, had nothing higher to expect from life than recognition as artists. They worked harder, and, as a group, were the ones who set a shining example for aspiring youngsters to follow.

**15**

JAN ABRAHAMSZ.
BEERSTRATEN (1622–1666)
*The Dam, Amsterdam, with
the old town hall, in the
snow.* Signed *J A Beere-
straten. f*. Panel, 49 × 59
cm.

Amsterdam, Amsterdams
Historisch Museum,
inv.nr. 39 (A 2999).
Purchased in 1874 from
W.A. Hopman,
Amsterdam.

As Albert Blankert has
pointed out, Dutch
paintings of old buildings
were often inspired by
demolition and disaster.
The old town hall of
Amsterdam provides
evidence for both parts
of his contention. The
building was in the course
of demolition when it
was destroyed by fire. The
mixture of contrary
emotions can well be
imagined. Depictions of
the old building are dis-
tinctly rare before the

1640s, when it suddenly
became the object of
solicitous attention by
artists. Their solicitousness
increased even more after
the fire. Beerstraten's
evocation of the building
would seem to be one of
those nostalgic ones which
were copied from old
drawings or prints, while
the town hall itself was in
ashes. It shows the roof as
it looked between 1615
and 1640, while the painting is probably from the
1650s.

For another of Beer-
straten's many snow
scenes, see cat.nr. 25.

Cat. Amsterdams Histo-
risch Museum 1975/1979,
nr. 39.

**16**

GERRIT LUNDENS (1622–ca. 1683)
*The fire in the old town hall, Amsterdam, 1652.* Signed and dated *G. Lundens 1652.* Panel, 29.5 × 33.5 cm.

Amsterdam, Amsterdams Historisch Museum, cat. nr. 255, inv. nr. B 4512. Acquired at the W. J. R. Dreesmann sale, Amsterdam (F. Muller), 22 March 1960, lot 523 (as Egbert van der Poel).

When Amsterdam welcomed Maria de' Medici in 1638, one of the founding professors of the Athenaeum, Caspar van Baerle, composed an official poetic description of the event. When he came to the old town hall, he wrote: 'Its antiquity and dilapidation lend the building a certain venerableness. A city which is otherwise so splendidly built shows here how simple she was of old.'

This symbol of what we might call Republican virtue was being replaced by a building of imperial pretension when fire did the work of the demolition crew at 2 o'clock in the morning of July 7, 1652. The city was abuzz with rumours of arson, and the mood was so tense that the burgomasters called out the guard to prevent looting.

Of course the fire was seen as an omen. On July

6, twelve Dutch men-o'-war had been sunk in the English Channel, the first act of overt hostility in the disastrous Anglo-Dutch War. The news must have reached Amsterdam in the course of the 7th, while the ashes of the town hall were still asmoulder. And there were those who saw the hand of God in the fire, a punishment to the impious town government, which was elevating itself above God's church

(see nr. 17). One artist who
felt that way, I believe,
was Cornelis de Bie, who
painted a picture of the fire
in 1653. Another artist
who painted it was Claes
Moyaert, who *was* in
sympathy with the town
council. The ruins were
drawn by Rembrandt and
drawn and painted by
Beerstraten.

Dudok van Heel 1976,
p. 34. Cat. Amsterdams
Historisch Museum 1975/

1979, nr. 255, and under
nr. 54. A. Blankert, review
of W. Stechow, *Dutch
landscape painting*, in
*Simiolus* 2 (1967/1968),
p. 106.

Fig. 3
JAN ABRAHAMSZ.
BEERSTRATEN
*The ruins of the old town
hall of Amsterdam after the
fire of July 7, 1652.* Canvas,
110 × 144 cm. Amsterdam,
Rijksmuseum (on loan to
the Amsterdams Historisch
Museum).

If painting the portraits of the mighty was a second-rate specialty that could be practiced by nearly anyone, there were other kinds of official commissions which carried more prestige and security from competition. By mastering complex subjects from literature, history and the Bible, an artist could automatically leave his brothers behind him. He who did so would find himself in a smaller, more select category than the masses of portraitists. Such 'paintings with a college education' were considered more than just another specialty. They were the sum of all specialties, and elevated the art of painting to a higher spiritual status. The ability to create good 'history paintings,' as they were called, made one eligible for another form of security: the respectful patronage of princes and governments.

Most of the works ordered by official bodies were of that kind, and were of a predictable nature. Altarpieces for churches or chapels, exemplary scenes of civic leadership and the administration of justice for town halls and courts of law; allegories of trade for guilds (see cat. nr. 32) and so forth.

Aside from such obvious examples, however, every once in a while one runs across a commission of a completely different nature, a painting one would never think of as official. One of the most intriguing puzzles of this kind is the *Monk squeezing the breast of a nun* (cat.nr. 11).

In 1591, the town of Haarlem bought the canvas from one of the most important painters in the city, Cornelis Cornelisz. van Haarlem, to be hung in the Prinsenhof, the Prince's Court. This was where the Prince of Orange would stay when he visited the city, and it was therefore an important public building.

The purchase of the painting was part of a combined order. The much larger work paid for at the same time was a monumental panel showing the Massacre of the Innocents, the slaughter of all two-year-old Jewish boys ordered by King Herod in the year 2, for the well-known reason. The new painting, nine by eight feet, was ordered by the city as a centrepiece for two wings painted nearly half a century earlier by Maerten van Heemskerk for the chapel of the drapers' guild in the main church of Haarlem, St. Bavo's.

During the siege of Haarlem at the start of the Eighty Years War, the panels were removed from the church, and in 1581 they became township property. Ten years later followed the decision to install them, with a new central panel by Cornelis, in the Prince's Court, a former monastery which had been confiscated from the Dominicans and given to the city in compensation for losses suffered during the Spanish siege. The bloody choice of the subject has been interpreted as a reference to the cruelty of the enemy.

But why did the township order the *Monk and nun* from Cornelis at the same time? One seemingly plausible answer is that the painting was intended to serve as a demonstration of the corruption of monastic life in the Catholic past. A kind of justification for seizing the building. If that theory is correct, the man

**17**

GERRIT ADRIAENSZ.
BERCKHEYDE (1638–1698)
*The town hall of Amsterdam.*
Signed *G. Berckheide.*
Canvas, 75.5 × 91 cm.

The Netherlands Office
for Fine Arts, inv.nr.NK
1978 (on loan to the prime
minister's official resi-
dence, the Catshuis).

The eighth wonder of the
world, as the Amster-
damers called their new
town hall, was a tourist-
trade favourite even before
it was finished. Souvenirs
of the building ranged
from catchpenny prints to
glorious paintings such as
this. The Haarlemer Gerrit
Berckheyde painted at
least twenty views of the
building between 1665 and
1694. He even paired it
with other symbols of
civic and national pride,
producing pendant 'por-
traits' of the Amsterdam
town hall with paintings
of the stadholder's quarter
in The Hague and the ca-
thedral of St. Bavo in
Haarlem.

The building and its
paintings were a symbol of
something else besides
civic pride: resistance to
church interference in
politics. The high-rising
dome (whose height is
always exaggerated by
Berckheyde) was an
abomination to the Cal-
vinists of Amsterdam,
who wanted to add an
even higher tower to the
neighboring New Church,
but were prevented from
doing so by the burgo-
masters. The denomina-
tional sympathy of an
artist or his patrons can be
read out of the relative
heights of the town hall
and the New Church in
views of the Dam. In
Berckheyde's, as in those
of Jan van der Heyden, the
town hall is always taller,
while a view by Cornelis
de Bie includes the pro-
jected tower of the church,
a tower never built,
looming impossibly large.

De Jongh 1973. Schwartz
1985, p.265.

and woman would be enjoying illicit sex as well as fruit and wine.

However, the opposite explanation has also been advanced: that the painting is a proof of purity. There was a Haarlem legend concerning a nun who was falsely accused of having borne a child in secret. To test the charge, a monk squeezed her breasts to see if milk would flow from them. Instead, they produced wine, the symbol of the eucharist. If *that* is the subject of the painting, then the figures are not in the throes of sexual excitement at all, but are participants in a solemn mystery.

The confiscation and refurbishing of the Prinsenhof provided the occasion for hanging up old paintings by Haarlem masters and ordering a few new ones. The construction of a completely new official building was often the motor behind truly large-scale commissions for paintings. The palaces of Frederik Hendrik, for instance, were decorated with hundreds of paintings, many of them commissioned or purchased from living Dutch artists.

The most prominent piece of civic architecture to arise in Holland in the seventeenth century was the new town hall of Amsterdam, built between 1648 and 1655 on the Dam, the square in the center of town that gave Amsterdam (the Dam on the Amstel) its name. The building was intended from the start as a showpiece of Amsterdam grandeur, to which all the arts contributed their share. Architects, sculptors, painters and poets devoted their talents over a period of decades to create a fitting seat and symbol for the city government. In those days, to borrow a phrase applied in the 1960s to the great multinational concerns, Amsterdam had global reach. Decisions taken on the Dam affected not only the fates of European nations, but also, through the East and West India Companies, the daily life of say a shopkeeper in Ceylon, a coolie in Batavia, a prostitute in Nagasaki, a tribe of Iroquois Indians.

Not much effort had to be expended to convince the burgomasters that the arts could enhance their status. They convinced themselves, as it were, when they observed the effects of the public festivities held in the city streets from time to time from the 1630s through the 1650s. Like many rulers throughout history, they thrilled to the sight of a vast public admiring the symbols of their greatness. They also liked the idea that works of art could outlive them, and proclaim their glory to the future.

One of the official poets of the city, Jan Vos, addressed these lines to the leading burgomaster, Cornelis de Graeff:

> Tired old Time, now pining for his rest,
> Was cast by Painting in a form so fresh
> That Death, consumer of all human flesh,
> Could not destroy it, through he tried his best.[2]

**18**

ROELOF KOETS (1655–1725)
*Joost Christoffer van Bevervoorde tot Oldemeule (ca. 1640-January 1, 1700), his wife Judith Margaretha van Coevorden tot Rhaen (d. 1702), and her son from an earlier marriage.* Canvas, 109.5 × 198.5 cm.

Enschede, Rijksmuseum Twenthe. Purchased by the museum in 1977 from Jonkheer B.F. van Bevervoorden, Castellina in Chianti, Italy. The last owner was not a descendant of the sitter.

Judith Margaretha was previously married to Zweder Christoffel Schele tot Weleveld, who died before March 15, 1663. Her two children from that marriage both died young, and her second marriage was barren. It was not unusual for the deceased to be included in family portraits, but in this painting the presence of one child seems to indicate that only Judith's still living son was portrayed.

The sitters are from titled families of the inland provinces, where the nobility was still represented as a class in government. The landed aristocrats of Holland and burghers with country estates began having themselves painted outdoors with their families in the early seventeenth century. This example is unusual for the strange emptiness of the central portion, where one expects a view of the manse. Its absence turns the distance between the loving couple and the lonesome child into a chasm.

Roelof Koets was the foremost portraitist of his time in Zwolle, the capital of Overijssel province. He had ties of various kinds with his colleague Gerard ter Borch in Deventer, the second city of the province.

Museum information. For marriage portraits, see de Jongh 1986.

The lines are from an epic poem whose main function seems to have been to recommend for city commissions a group of Amsterdam painters who were Vos's friends.

Most artists in Amsterdam rose to the challenge enthusiastically, but there were always cynics on the sidelines who liked to remind people that the marriage of art and politics had its sordid side. One of them was the satirical poet Mattheus Gansneb Tengnagel, who wrote this squib when the plans for the new town hall were first announced in 1640:

ON THE TOWN HALL TO BE

Wealth the boss and art the slave unite
To build a Temple to God-given right.[3]

As Tengnagel sees it, the artists were flunkies helping their masters build a monument to their own divine right to rule. If there was any poet in Amsterdam who would recognize the phenomenon when he saw it, it would be Tengnagel. His father Jan had been portrait painter to some of the most important politicians in Amsterdam before he was appointed deputy sheriff and abandoned painting.

During the building of the new town hall, the old one, a venerable medieval landmark, burned down by accident before it could be demolished (cat.nrs. 15, 16). Amsterdam was shocked into an attack of civic nostalgia. One of the paintings hung in the burgomasters' chamber of the new building was a 'portrait' of the old one by the greatest specialist of the day, Pieter Saenredam. The building was also decorated generously with allegories of good government from the Bible and the classics, and with a monumental series on the revolt of the Batavians, the forefathers of the Dutch, against the Romans.

Then, of course, there were the paintings of the new building itself, dozens if not hundreds of them. The one by Gerrit Berckheyde (cat.nr. 17) shows it after completion, a magnificent monument of modernity in its classical details and structure.

It was two hundred and thirty years before a larger building than the town hall was erected in Amsterdam – the Rijksmuseum. If the art of painting was an appendage to the building of the town hall, it was the main reason for building the Rijksmuseum. However, the art hung in the town hall was made by living masters, and that in the Rijksmuseum mainly by dead ones, including the same masters who worked for the burgomasters in the 1650s.

In The Hague, paintings were displayed in transformed palaces and private galleries. The Mauritshuis, built in the 1640s for Johan Maurits, the stadholder's nephew, was bought by the State in 1820 to house the newly founded Royal

**19**

HENDRIK POTHOVEN
(1728-1793)
*The main hall of the
Binnenhof with the State
Lottery.* Signed and dated
*HPothoven P A° 1779.*
Canvas, 57 × 65.7 cm.

The Hague, Mauritshuis,
inv.nr. 764. Bequest of
J.G. de Groot Jamin,
Amsterdam, 1921.

The Binnenhof, like many
another public building in
the Republic, was not
treated with excessive
deference by the govern-
ment that owned it. The
antiquity and historical
importance of the main
hall did not prevent the
States General from
making it available, from
1709 on, for the drawings
of the national lottery.

Van Gelder 1937, p.208.

Gallery of Paintings. And in 1840, King Willem II, an amateur architect, built a Gothic Hall (in the English Perpendicular Style) for the display of his own collection of old masters. At the time, he said that he intended to put up another Hall for his modern paintings, but he never did get around to it.

1. The artist-officeholders I have come across so far are, by province:

FRIESLAND: Jacobus Sibrand Mancadam (Franeker and Leeuwarden); Adriaen van Cronenburgh (Tietjerksteradeel); Willem Bartel van der Kooi (Achtkarspelen).

HOLLAND: Gillis Anthonisz. Beth and Jan Tengnagel (Amsterdam); Aelbert Cuyp (Dordrecht); Jacob van der Ulft and Hendrik Verschuring (Gorinchem); Pieter van Veen, Seger Crijnsz. van der Maes and Dirk van der Lisse (The Hague); Isaac Claesz. van Swanenburg, Pieter van Veen and Jan Adriaensz. van Staveren (Leiden); Jacob Lois (Rotterdam); Gijsbert Sibilla (Weesp).

OVERIJSSEL: Gerard ter Borch (Zwolle).

UTRECHT: Paulus Moreelse (Utrecht).

ZEELAND: Dirck van Delen (Arnemuiden).

2. Vos 1653, p. 30.
3. 'Op het Toekomende Raedhuis. De Rijkdom, en de konst, die meester, deeze knecht,/Zijn uit op Tempelbouw voor 't Goddelijke recht.' Tengnagel 1969, p. 292.

# Religion

'Dutch Calvinism' conjures up an image of a nation of pious churchgoers predestined for heaven, smug about it and taking grim pleasure in the prospect of all Papists, infidels and sinners going to hell. We imagine sparsely furnished, scrubbed interiors, selfdenying men and women dressed in black. Bodies, souls, a whole society dedicated to a dour God. The phrase and the image are both so hackneyed that a writer with any claim to originality will want to deflate them as pointedly as possible. Looking more closely, one finds that there is little honour to be had from the exercise. One doesn't even need to brandish a point – a poke of the finger is enough to puncture the cliché, at least as it is applied to the Dutch people as a whole.

Calvinism came to Holland in the Reformation, and captured the hearts of a small part of the population. Many of the Dutch, unhappy with the moral and material abuses of the Catholic church, were eager to join reformed churches, of which Calvinism was one. An estimated ten to twenty percent of the population became Calvinist in the sixteenth century, a figure that increased in later centuries, but never reached fifty percent. What distinguished Calvinism from other Protestant sects is that the others were either too extreme in their politics or too respectful of authority to gain much influence. Calvinism had the right mixture of rebelliousness and authoritativeness to replace Catholicism as a new orthodoxy. In the course of the 1560s and '70s, the governments of the Dutch cities underwent an 'alteration,' in which Catholic officeholders were replaced by Calvinists.

This was part of the beginning of the Eighty Years War of the northern Netherlands against Spain, and it shook Dutch society from top to bottom. Outside the church and government, one of the groups that was shaken most thoroughly were the artists. This was a function not of any social, political or religious peculiarities of artists as a group, but of the nature of their 'product.' Perhaps the most conspicuous difference between the Catholics and the Calvinists was in their attitude towards art in the church. Religious images considered an adjunct to divine service by the Catholics were idols to the Calvinists. Throughout the southern provinces, and here and there in the north, the revolt of the Netherlands was marked by outbreaks of iconoclasm: the breaking of images. Groups of Calvinist activists, often joined by mobs from the street, went into the churches and stripped them of their art. Statues of the saints were tumbled from their pedestals and altarpieces were slashed to shreds,

**20**

THOMAS DE KEYSER
(1596-1667)
*A Dutch patriarch in the guise of Moses being shown the promised land by an angel, with three members of his family (?).* Panel, 51 × 76 cm.

The Netherlands Office for Fine Arts, inv.nr.NK 1494 (on loan to Rijksmuseum Het Catharijneconvent, Utrecht). Confiscated by the Germans from the Jewish Amsterdam art dealer Jacques Goudstikker. The confiscation was one of the first acts of the army of occupation; a special unit was sent to Holland expressly to seize the Goud-stikker stock. The art dealer himself was able, with his wife, to get onto a ship for England, but during the crossing he fell into an open hold and was killed.

Holland is one of the many Christian nations which identified itself with the Chosen People, as it also identified itself with ancient Rome. Individuals too would take on roles from the Bible or from classical authors to give symbolic meaning to some important aspect of their lives. In occasional poetry – verse written for some specific event, such as a marriage, a birth or a death – the subject of the poem is cast more often than not in literary or historical disguise. The same would sometimes be done in painting. Here we see an unknown Dutch family, acting the part, it is thought, of Israelites looking at the promised land. Perhaps the younger generation was returning to their country after a period in exile, for religious reasons, and wished to commemorate the father who had died abroad, comparing him to Moses, who was not allowed by God to cross the Jordan into the land of Israel. However, a proper interpretation of the painting will only be possible if we learn more about the sitters and the circumstances of the commission.

It should not be automatically assumed that the sitters were Calvinists. Other Protestant groups, such as the Remonstrants and the Mennonites, identified themselves just as strongly with the Israelites, to the exclusion of the Calvinists. And Thomas de Keyser is also known to have been patronized by Amsterdam Catholics, many of whom went into exile in the 1580s and only returned to the city in the course of the seventeenth century.

in the name of combatting idolatry. Campaigns of this kind have taken place at other points in history, and for different reasons: in the Byzantine Empire in the eighth century, for the sake of Christian orthodoxy; in England during the Civil War, and during the French and Russian Revolutions, out of antagonism towards the church and the old regime; in China during the Cultural Revolution, to break the hold of the past on the popular imagination. What these occurrences have in common, in our eyes, is what one could call spiritual terrorism. Those who perform it – more often than not governments – realize that they are touching a particularly sensitive nerve of society with maximum effect, and for a minimum of effort and risk.

(One English iconoclast of the 1640s, William Dowsing, kept a journal which contains calm, bureaucratic reports of activities that make our blood run cold. On January 6, 1643, he noted: 'We broke down about an hundred superstitious pictures and seven Fryars hugging a Nunn; and the Picture of God and Christ; and diverse others very superstitious... and we beat down a great stoneing Cross on the top of the Church.'[1] I quote this for the fascinating reference to a painting of seven friars 'hugging' a nun, which sounds so much like the painting by Cornelis van Haarlem (cat.nr.11) which was ordered by the town of Haarlem in the wake of its own iconoclasm. Could it be that a similar painting was destroyed in Haarlem?)

Whatever the motives of the Netherlandish iconoclasts, one effect of their acts was to tumble sacred art itself from its pedestal. A part of daily life which was cherished by Christians for centuries could never again be taken for granted. When the Catholic church was re-established in the southern Netherlands, the cult of images returned with it, but in a more self-conscious, carefully controlled form.

In the north, where the Calvinists gained control of the existing churches, the old paintings and statues never returned, nor were new ones ordered. In the Calvinist hierarchy of psycho-spiritual values, the ear took precedence over the eye, the sermon over the painted (let along graven) image. The proper vehicle for transmitting the message of God was the Word. Visual images were fit only to inspire baser feelings, for which the churchgoer had no need. The only paintings one saw on the walls of a Calvinist church were boards with coats of arms or texts like the Ten Commandments, in gold on black – painted, more often than not, over the image of a saint or a Bible story.

To artists, this entailed the loss of the largest single market for their work, at a time when their numbers were being swelled immensely by immigration. But the banning of images from the churches also raised more profound issues. In the Catholic world, many artists are, after all, respected servants of the church, with all the status that brings. The images they make excite feelings of religious devotion, which sometimes can approach idolatry in their intensity.

**21**

CLAES MOYAERT (1591–1665)
*The Catholic priest Leonard Marius (1588-1652).*
Painted in 1647. Panel, 122.5 × 89 cm.

Utrecht, Rijksmuseum Het Catharijneconvent, inv. nr. St. CC s.24. Purchased at sale Amsterdam (Sotheby Mak van Waay), December 13, 1982, lot 359a.

Although the Dutch Catholics were prohibited from practicing their religion in public, they made every attempt to keep the structure of the pre-Reformation church intact. This difficult task was not made any easier by the proximity of the southern Netherlands, with its flourishing Catholic life and promising career opportunities for ecclesiastics. The gifted preacher Marius nearly became court chaplain to Archduchess Isabella, daughter of Philip II, but was sent instead in 1630 to the hostile northern Netherlands as vicar-general of the former bishopric of Haarlem. He was also rector of the Beguinage (Begijnhof) in Amsterdam, the nerve centre of Catholic life in the city. Marius was able to bring many an apostate back to the mother church. The most spectacular conversion in his period was that of Joost

van den Vondel. Whether or not Marius or, as another version of the story goes, a Catholic widow deserves the credit is a moot point, but it is certain that the poet admired Marius, to whom he dedicated two poems.

As the leading Catholic painter of Amsterdam in this period, Claes Moyaert was the portraitist of preference to his co-religionists. He painted Marius at least three times during his life, and once on his bier.

After Marius's death, this portrait was published by Dirk Matham in a engraving, with the following inscription by Vondel:

Thus did Marius edify the
   lettered and unschooled
   alike
By spoken words and
   written, with zeal
   inspired by God.
Now he speaks no more,
   now his golden pen lies
   still.
The liveliest image of him
   is what he left in print.

The verbal play between word and image, written and visual record, is a constant feature of poems of this kind – and also of many paintings. Moyaert too was looking for a means of showing Marius as a writer and speaker. The strongest impression is made on us, however, not by his spiritual gifts but by his striking personal appearance.

The ebony frame is original. It is an early example of a frame with a concave profile.

NNBW, vol. 7, cols. 839–840. Vondel, vol. 5, p. 552. Dudok van Heel 1976. Exhib. cat. *Prijst de lijst*, p. 154.

As the creator of objects which are seen by many as mediators between man and God, the artist himself is a kind of priest. If painters were distinguished from their fellow craftsmen by any one aspect of their profession, this was it. One can imagine how traumatic it must have been for the painters of sixteenth-century Holland to see the spiritual superiority of their work turned into its opposite. What was once a mark of distinction became a sign of shame.

The most extreme response to this reversal of values was that of the Zeeland artist Marinus van Roemerswaele, who at the end of his life participated in the iconoclastic riots in Middelburg. There must have been others like him who repented of their former lives and turned against art. But they were not typical. Most artists, even those who were staunch Calvinists, felt an instinctive horror for iconoclasm, and showed it. Carel van Mander gave expression to the general feeling when he called the iconoclasts 'maniacs.' Not that he argued for the return of sacred art to the churches. He himself was a Protestant, and a refugee from Spanish misrule. He was also too realistic to expect the restoration of art to the church, and too prudent to suggest it. Van Mander had other ideas for undoing the worst damage done to the artist by the Reformation. The loss of the church as patron could be made good by wealthy individuals (in Dutch a patron of the arts is called a 'Maecenas,' after the protector of Virgil and Horace) and by civil governments. As for the spiritual status of the artist, this could be raised to its former height by the practice of 'history painting' at a high intellectual and moral level.

Van Mander's solution remained the canonical one, and was repeated with variations by later writers on art. But it was not the only one. For one thing, not all the churches in the world were Calvinist. Flanders and parts of Germany were still Catholic, and there were Lutheran countries where art was still tolerated in the church. Dutch artists could move to these neighbouring parts of Christendom, as some did. Italy was further afield, yet hundreds of Dutch artists went there, sometimes for years at a time. The reason most often given for the trip south was pedagogical: how could an aspiring young Dutch artist better acquaint himself with the great models of ancient and Renaissance art than by going to Rome? But more than one such aspiring young artist remained until he turned gray, working not in the style of the ancients or of Raphael but in that of the latest trendsetters in modern Italian painting, artists like Caravaggio and Adam Elsheimer. Some adopted the new styles so successfully that their work is still indistinguishable from Italian art of the same period. Colonies of northern artists were a fixture in all the important centres of Italian art, especially Rome. Many of the denizens of that notoriously Bohemian world were Catholics when they came to Italy, or converted once they were there. Rembrandt's first master, Jacob Isaacsz. van Swanenburgh, the son of Isaac Claesz. (see cat. nr. 1), is an example. He lived in Naples for over a

**22**

PAULUS BOR (ca. 1600–
1669)
*The finding of Moses.*
Painted in the latter 1630s.
Canvas, 132.5 × 115.5 cm.

Amsterdam, Rijks-
museum, inv. nr. A 852.

From the house of Con-
stantijn Huygens, The
Hague, 1874.

Bor was one of a small
group of artists from
Amersfoort, in Utrecht
province, who enjoyed the
favour of Frederik

Hendrik thanks to the old
friendship between the
stadholder's secretary
Constantijn Huygens and
Joannes Brosterhuysen,
who lived for a time on
the estate of the most
important of the Amers-
foort group, Jacob van

Campen. Van Campen
was introduced to Huy-
gens by Brosterhuysen in
1632, and soon became the
stadholder's architect.
   The painting style of the
Amersfoorters was sophis-
tication itself masquerad-
ing as simplicity. Broster-

huysen was a humanistic scholar, and his friends were all quite learned. Once, in 1645, sending Huygens a drawing he had made of the town of Amersfoort with the van Campen estate, he added a note saying 'I know that you do not make much of painters' dreams and whimseys, but cherish work done from life or drawn from the object itself.' Even in a biblical subject such as this, Bor tried to create an impression of that kind of directness. His tactic was to avoid stock figures and stereotypes, to work from local living models, to rethink his subjects rigorously and to reduce visible artifice to a minimum.

This painting comes from the house of Constantijn Huygens in The Hague, and was probably made for him. In 1827, and perhaps in Huygens's lifetime as well, it hung above the door of one of the smaller rooms, opposite an interior of the church of St. Mary, Utrecht, by Pieter Saenredam. Saenredam was a Haarlem friend of van Campen's, and it can be illuminating to look at his church paintings in the context of the artistic ideas of the Amersfoorters.

Worp 1911, pp.379-380. Worp 1915, pp.160-161. Bloch 1949. Lunsingh Scheurleer 1962, pp.180-181.

quarter-century before returning home, after his father's death, with a Catholic wife whose existence he had kept secret for seventeen years. He had been working as a painter and running a shop for artists' supplies in Naples.

But there were alternatives closer to home. Not all the churches of Holland were Calvinist. Catholicism was never suppressed completely, and masses were still being held in Amsterdam and Utrecht and The Hague. Catholics were forbidden to pray in buildings that looked like churches from the outside, but they became skilled in turning townhouses into 'secret' places of worship that could accommodate hundreds. It seems certain that many paintings of religious subjects by Dutch artists of the seventeenth century were made for clandestine Catholic churches or for the homes of Catholic priests and laymen. This is a poorly documented area of art history, and a disputed one. Every once in a while, however, one comes across a piece of fairly incontrovertible evidence. The inventory of the goods of the Amsterdam painter Dirck Aertsz. falls into that category. When he died in 1644, the paintings he left behind included a large number of Madonnas, altarpieces, series of the twelve apostles, saints and other paintings that were clearly intended for use in Catholic worship.[2] Not all of them were made for the home market, it would seem. Quite a few are painted on copper plates, which van Mander tells us were the kind of paintings that Spaniards liked to buy when they left the southern Netherlands for home.[3]

Another denomination whose members had a penchant for religious art of a particular kind were the Mennonites. These were the followers of the Frisian Anabaptist Menno Simons. Their creed was just as unpopular with the more middle-of-the-road Reformed churches as it was with the Catholics. Although they had no theological dispute with the Calvinists concerning the evils of idolatry, they seem to have been less worried about their faith being perverted by religious images. One of the more intriguing Mennonites in Dutch art was the Leeuwarden painter and art dealer Lambert Jacobsz., who was actually the leader of his congregation. (The very idea of a Calvinist divine being a professional painter seems impossible). By the eighteenth century the Mennonites had established a leading position in Dutch cultural life. From their midst came Pieter Teyler, who turned his own collection of art, scientific instruments and natural history into a museum, and donated his fortune to a foundation. Both still survive, a testimony to the commitment of Teyler and his successors. Even if one can speak of a certain Mennonite proclivity towards art, however, there is no kind of painting that can be called typically Mennonite.

Greater tolerance towards religious art was also demonstrated by a Calvinist schism known as Remonstrantism, which played a major role in Dutch religious politics, especially in the 1610s. The basic point of doctrinal contention

**23**

COPY AFTER REMBRANDT
VAN RIJN (1606-1669)
*Christ appearing to the
Magdalene as a gardener*
(John 20:14-17). Panel,
62 × 51 cm.

The Netherlands Office
for Fine Arts, inv.nr.NK
1648 (on loan to Museum
Amstelkring, Amsterdam).
Before the war in the Katz
Gallery, Dieren.

The original, in Buck-
ingham Palace, is dated
1638. If one draws a dis-
tinction between Rem-
brandt's 'public' paintings,
which were known to a
good many art lovers, and
the 'private' ones which
disappeared into a closed
collection or crossed the
border as soon as they
were made, the original of
this painting certainly
belongs to the former
category.
  This poem by Jeremias
de Decker, from the early
1650s, is attached to the
back of the painting in
Buckingham Palace:

When I read St. John's
  description of this scene
And turn to see it in this
  splendid painting, then
I ask myself if brush has
  ever followed pen
As aptly, or dead paint so
  near to life has been.

Christ seems to say 'Marie,
  don't tremble, I am
  here,
It's me. Your master's free
  of Death's authority'

Believing, though not yet
    with all her heart and
    mind, she
Seems poised between her
    joy and grief, her hope
    and fear.

As art dictates, the tomb's
    a tall and rocky tower,
Rich with shade, thus
    lending sightliness and
    power
To all the rest. Because,
    friend Rembrandt, I
    once saw
This panel undergo your
    deft and expert touch,
I wished to rhyme a verse
    on your most gifted
    brush,
To add praise with my ink
    to the paints with which
    you draw.

As in Vondel's verse of
1652 on the portrait of
the late Leonard Marius
(cat.nr.20), the poet
compares writing – the
Bible text – with pictorial
depiction – Rembrandt's
representation of that text.
He pays Rembrandt the
great compliment of
having followed his text as
well as any artist ever had.
To us, this may sound like
scant praise, but in the
seventeenth century poetry
stood in much higher
esteem than painting. And
the Bible, after all, is the
Bible.

Schwartz 1985, pp.182,
340-341. Schatborn 1985,
pp.50-51.

between the Remonstrants and the adherents of the 'true Christian Reformed religion,' as the Calvinists called themselves, concerned predestination: the dogma that God determines the fate of each individual before his or her birth. By rejecting the more extreme forms of this belief (some Calvinists held that God decided before the creation of the universe which future humans were to go to heaven and which to hell), the Remonstrants brought down on themselves charges of Papistry and denying divine omnipotence. In fact, Remonstrantism did occupy an uneasy middle ground between Protestantism and Catholicism. This was just as evident in their more easy-going attitude towards art as in their theology.

Having said all this, it must be stressed that despite their history of iconoclasm and a continuing equivocation in their attitude towards art, the Calvinists remained the most important group in the country, in whose circles we find the major collectors and patrons of the arts. Moreover, the social and professional boundaries between the various sects were not that sharply drawn. As the English ambassador in the Netherlands, Sir William Temple, remarked in 1688: 'It is hardly to be imagined, how all the violence and sharpness, which accompanies the differences of Religion in other Countrys, seems to be appeased or softned here, by the general freedom which all men enjoy...'[4] We have already noted that in his Lives of the Artists, Carel van Mander avoided talking about the government positions of artists. He also avoided talking about their religion. That he himself was probably a Mennonite has to be deduced from outside evidence.[5] Membership of a particular congregation naturally gave an artist better chances to work for his co-religionists than an outsider (van Mander designed the title prints of the Bibles published by the leading Mennonite printer, for example), but there was nothing to be gained in making the fact known to others. Sectarianism in matters of religion was bad for business. And dangerous. Johannes Torrentius, who claimed that his Rosicrucianism gave him magical powers as an artist, ended up in prison. He lost the 'general freedom which all men enjoy' by insisting too strongly on his specialness.

This public reticence in matters of religion disappeared in the nineteenth century, when Catholicism came back into the open, and everyone had to stand up and be counted. The religious art of that age often does betray the adherence of its maker to one or another of the prevailing denominations.

One of the great concessions that the Calvinists won from the States General was ownership of all the churches in the country. On the one hand, this was a nearly mandatory consequence of the recognition of Calvinism as the 'public church' (not the state church), but on the other, it was downright unhandy. The churches of the Netherlands had been built during the middle ages for the

**24**

AERT DE GELDER (1645–1727)
*Edna blessing Tobias.*
Signed *A. de Gelder f.*
Canvas, 88 × 112 cm.

The Netherlands Office for Fine Arts, inv. nr. NK 1909 (on loan to the Groninger Museum). From the Goudstikker gallery (see nr. 19).

The young Tobias was sent by his father Tobit on a mission to his distant relative Raguel. Accompanied by the angel Raphael in disguise, he was able, arriving at his destination, to cure Raguel's daughter Sarah of a curse and claim her as his bride, along with half of Raguel's property. Upon the departure of Tobias and Sarah, Raguel blessed the couple, 'And Edna said to Tobias, "The Lord of Heaven bring you back safely, dear brother, and grant me to see your children by my daughter Sarah, that I may rejoice before the Lord. See, I am entrusting my daughter to you; do nothing to grieve her"' (Tobit 10:12).

The book of Tobit has an appeal that goes beyond pure religion. Tobias's peregrinations in the company of an angel made him a guardian for all travelers, especially young ones, and the miracles he performed had something homely and comforting to them. The book was mistrusted by the Calvinists, however, who included it in the official Dutch Bible translation of 1636 only grudgingly. In art, it is most often depicted by artists with connections to the Mennonite and Catholic communities, who were especially attached to the book. In the 1620s and '30s, when Rembrandt was working closely with dissident Protestants in Leiden and Amsterdam, he painted subjects from Tobit several times. He, his pupils and associates turned to Tobit more frequently than any other group of Dutch painters.

Aert de Gelder was Rembrandt's last pupil, coming from Dordrecht to work under him in the 1660s. He acquired and retained some of the most personal techniques of the late Rembrandt, continuing to put them into practice

entire populations of cities and their surroundings, at a time when there was only one cult in Christendom. Now they came into the hands of a minority group which moreover was very strict about who was welcome to pray with them. And the Dutch were not such great churchgoers to begin with. The Englishman Fynes Moryson, visiting Holland in 1593, noted in his journal that the churches were 'seldom full, for very many Sectaryes, and more marchants proeffering gayne to the dutyes of Religion, seldome came to Church, so as in Leyden a populous Citty, I often observed at tymes of divine service, much more people to be in the markett place than in the Church.'[5]

After iconoclasm, the churches were as devoid of decoration as of people (Moryson found them 'without beauty on the insyde'), and for the first half-century of the Republic were a loss to the art of painting. A turning point came in 1627, with the creation of a new genre, the church portrait. The Haarlem artist Pieter Saenredam was at work on the illustrations for a book on his home town. One of them was a view of the interior of the church of St. Bavo, the former cathedral, on the main square. Saenredam, as systematic and scrupulous an artist as ever lived, sat himself down in the middle of the nave and drew a perfectly symmetrical perspective view of the church. For the print, he added a congregation, the lonely little crowd Moryson leads us to expect, standing and sitting on temporary 'formes sett about the Pulpitt in the naked body of the Church.' A twelve-line poem in the lower margin asks us to admire the building for the way its elements seem to grow out of each other, and to respect it as a place where 'sound and pure doctrine' is taught.[6]

A year later, Saenredam used the drawing as the basis for a painting of exactly the same view.[7] Instead of the worshippers, however, the interior is now occupied by a small number of wealthy burghers parading through the building in their Sunday best. The impulse behind the creation of the painting was probably not far removed from that for the drawing and print: a manifestation of civic pride, enriched with antiquarian interest, aesthetic admiration and religion. There may even have been a Calvinist strain of dogmatism implied: the 'sound and pure doctrine' of the author of the book on Haarlem, the minister Samuel Ampzing, was of the harsh Counter-Remonstrant variety.

The whitewashed, undecorated interiors of the churches of Holland provided the ideal backdrop for sentiments and messages of many kinds. Saenredam himself made one painting, for example, which embodies a theological message devised by the first owner of the painting – Constantijn Huygens, Frederik Hendrik's secretary.[8] Other artists imbued their church interiors with national as well as civic and religious feeling: the painters of the New Church in Delft often managed to include in their views the famous grave monument of William of Orange, the father of his country. Ruminations on life and death

until well into the eighteenth century. One of these is what we might call the iconographical technique of painting biblical scenes in a semi-modern mode, with a heavy emphasis on emotion and expression, and as few attributes as possible.

are evoked by church interiors that include open graves (the dead were still buried beneath the church floor in the seventeenth century) and gravediggers, with or without the skulls of Dutch Yoricks.

One of the exceptional aspects of church portraiture is that it beautified the medieval past. Today the middle ages and its relics are one of the most popular aspects of western culture, but in the seventeenth century that was far from being the case. The architects of Holland were dismayed by all those vast outmoded hulks of churches whose overcapacity stood in the way of new commissions for churches in the classicistic style that was sweeping Europe. They missed no opportunity to cast a slur on the 'senseless Gothic curlicues' of the old churches. One of these critics was the amateur architect that Huygens also was, and it is a special tribute to Saenredam that his painting of one of those Gothic monsters hung above a doorway of Huygens's classicistic new house (see below, under cat.nr.22).

Another painter favoured by Huygens was the young Rembrandt. Around the time that Saenredam began making his church paintings, Rembrandt was commissioned by Huygens and his master Frederik Hendrik to paint a series of religious paintings for the stadholder's cabinet in The Hague. They depicted the passion of Christ – the Raising of the Cross, the Descent from the Cross, the Ascension, Entombment and Resurrection – and were based on famous paintings of the past by Titian and Rubens. Huygens recognized Rembrandt's unique talent for depicting emotions, and wished to help the young artist develop a new mode of religious art that would bring glory to the Dutch court. However, the relationship was not a lasting one. For reasons that had more to do with politics and personalities than clashing opinions on art, the patron and painter grew apart. It was in his work for the patricians of Amsterdam that Rembrandt created the biblical paintings that are regarded by many as the greatest works of religious art ever made.

In the subjects of some of them, there is a hint of sectarianism. For instance, in the 1620s and '30s and again in the 1650s, Rembrandt painted scenes taken from the book of Tobit. (See the painting by Rembrandt's late pupil Aert de Gelder, cat.nr.24.) This apocryphal book was the object of a dispute between the Calvinists and all the other Dutch denominations. In the new Calvinist Bible translation, the States Version, Tobit was preceded by a belittling 'Warning to the Reader' which said that it was being printed only in order to avoid controversy. The controversy was with the Mennonites in particular, who had a special affection for the book. It seems likely that Rembrandt made his paintings of Tobit for patrons who were not Calvinists, and that they had a somewhat provocative character. If so, they have long since lost that part of their meaning for the observer. Instead of provocative sectarianism, they have come to stand for a universal religiousness that does not shut out any kind of

**25**

JAN ABRAHAMSZ.
BEERSTRATEN (1622–1666)
*The church of Sloten in the
winter.* Signed *J. Beerstra...*
Painted in 1658 or 1659.
Canvas, 90 × 128 cm.

Amsterdam, Rijks-
museum, inv.nr. A 4134.
Presented by Miss S.E.
Dribbel, Amsterdam,
1967.

Sloten, now part of
metropolitan Amsterdam,
was a village in the
seventeenth century, under
a lord of the manor
appointed by the city of
Amsterdam. From 1650
until 1664, this position
was occupied by Cornelis
de Graeff, the most in-
fluential man in the city.
In the 1660s, the church
was restored with his help.

Nearly all of Beerstra-
ten's views are in the
snow. See also above,
nr. 14.

Another version of this
painting, in the Metropolitan Museum of Art, New
York, is believed to be a
copy by Beerstraten's son,
about whom we know
next to nothing.

Van Thiel 1968.

**26**

JOHANNES (JAN) WEISSENBRUCH (1822–1880)
*The church of St. Lawrence, Rotterdam.* Signed *J. Weissenbruch f.* Panel, 24.5 × 33 cm.

The Hague, Mesdag Museum, inv.nr. 336. Purchased by H.W. Mesdag for two hundred guilders at sale van de Heuvell et al., The Hague (Boussod), 16 November 1897, lot 89.

In 1863, the artist displayed a larger version of this scene, on canvas, at the annual Exhibition of Living Artists. That work, for which the panel in the Mesdag Museum appears to be a study, is said to have been painted about 1846. That would place the origin of this painting before the restoration of the church in 1853–1863.

The Sint Laurenskerk is the main church of Reformed Rotterdam, as it was that of Catholic Rotterdam before the Reformation. Its tower, begun in 1449, was completed in 1620 according to new designs by Hendrick de Keyser, but had to be demolished in 1645 on account of structural weakness. A few years later the rebuilt tower, in a breathtaking operation, was set up straight after it had leaned three-and-a-half feet to the northeast during a heavy storm. In the German bombardment of Rotterdam on May 14, 1940, the church was burnt out, but remained standing. Its restoration after the war was a symbol of Rotterdam's resuscitation.

Hazewinkel 1975, pp. 1040–1042. Van Schendel 1975, p. 170.

believer. They do not even shut out non-believers. In the universality of their appeal, they speak to each in his own tongue, of the things he holds most dear.

The nearly sacred humanism of Rembrandt's art is certainly one of the most enduring values attached to Dutch art. The phenomenon points up an intriguing historical truth. After iconoclasm, as we saw, the artists of Holland worried about the moral standing of their pursuit. Art derived so much of its worth to the Christian world from its subservience to religion that thinkers like van Mander were afraid that a secular art of painting would be indistinguishable to the burgher from the 'arts' of carpentry and glassmaking.

The worm has turned. Religion, in the past centuries, has been put on the defensive, while art – with Rembrandt in the fore – has held its own and more as a spiritual value in our culture. The reversal had gone halfway by 1880, when Vincent van Gogh, the son of a Reformed minister who had decided to devote his life to humanity through art, wrote in a letter to his brother: 'Someone loves Rembrandt, but seriously – that man will know there is a God, he will surely believe it.... To try to understand the real significance of what the great artists, the serious masters, tell us in their masterpieces, *that* leads to God.'[9] In the hundred years since, the attempt to understand the great artists has gained so much importance, and godliness has lost so much, that van Gogh's words now sound almost patronizing towards Rembrandt.

1. Quoted in Freedberg 1985, p.41, note 10.
2. Bredius 1915-1921, vol.2, The Hague 1916, pp.601-609.
3. Miedema 1981, p.38.
4. Temple 1693, p.205.
5. Jacobsen Jensen 1918, p.282.
6. Exhib. cat. *Pieter Jansz. Saenredam*, Utrecht 1961, nr.31.
7. *De Bavo te boek* 1985, p.83, in a chapter by Pieter Biesboer on paintings of the church. Until recently the painting, in the Philadelphia Museum of Art, was thought to have been made around 1635. A recent restoration revealed the date 1628.
8. Schwartz 1966-1967.
9. Van Gogh, vol.1, p.198 (letter 133).

**27**

WERNER VAN DEN
VALCKERT (ca. 1580–
ca. 1630)
*Family group as Caritas,
with self-portrait; in the
background, St. John the
Baptist preaching*. Inscribed
on the sheet of paper *Ick
heb dit... int Iaer ons heeren
1623... September in
Amstelredam*. Interpreted
by van Thiel as: I com-
pleted this in the year of
our Lord 1623 on Sep-
tember 10th in Amster-
dam. Panel, 162 × 125.5
cm. Cut down on the
right by about 49 cm.

The Netherlands Office
for Fine Arts, inv.nr.NK
1785. From the collections
of W. Peech, Amsterdam
and Dr. Keulens, Ander-
lecht.

The painting was known
to Arnold Houbraken in
1718, but he does not say
where he saw it, or who
the figures are. It is closely
related to another family
portrait by van den
Valckert, dated 1620,
which also includes a self-
portrait, and shows the
Amsterdam Catholic
patrician Michiel Poppen
and his family as participants in the Bible story of
Christ and the little
children. 'Now they were
bringing even infants to
him that he might touch
them; and when the dis-
ciples saw it, they rebuked
them. But Jesus called to
them saying, "Let the
children come to me, and

do not hinder them; for to
such belongs the kingdom
of God. Truly, I say to
you, whoever does not
receive the kingdom of
God like a child shall not
enter it"'(Luke 18:15-17;
see also Matthew 19:13-15
and Mark 10:13-16).

Our painting would
seem to convey a related
message. A woman sur-
rounded by children is
a figure of charity or
Christian love; the message
of John the Baptist in-
cludes the exhortation to
charity: 'He who has two
coats, let him share with
him who has none; and he
who has food, let him do
likewise' (Luke 3:11). The
common ideal expressed
in both works is that of
the Christian who opens
his heart to the needs of
others, and thereby earns
admittance to the king-
dom of heaven. Similar
sentiments, evoked with
comparable means, can be
found in the depiction of
public charity by Jan de
Bray (cat.nr.29) and that
of familial love by Nico-
laes Verkolje (cat.nr.88).

# Charity

It was a great disappointment to the Calvinists that they failed to gain control of *all* the former property of the Catholic church. They were given the old cathedrals and parish churches, but not, as a rule, the monasteries and convents. Of the hospitals and old age homes that before the alteration had been owned and run by the church, only a few ended up under official Calvinist auspices. The new church also failed to acquire the extensive real-estate holdings of the Catholics outside the cities, the income of which was used to finance charitable institutions. The States General deemed it wiser to confiscate these holdings for the townships rather than the church. Because of this far-reaching decision, the Calvinist church was prevented from the start from taking over the all-pervasive role that Catholicism previously filled in Dutch society.

The townships, for their part, were not equipped to run the institutions of health and welfare as divisions of government, and had no desire to do so. Rather than assuming direct, city-wide responsibility for the welfare of the orphaned, the aged, the sick and the needy, they committed them to the care of boards of burgher regents, such as those that already ran other, non-church charities. The regents would supervise the institution's estates, invest its funds and use them for the good of their wards. The day-to-day running of the institutions was left up to paid administrators.

In general, the members of the governing boards were appointed for life by co-optation, and came, needless to say, from the richest families. They saw their function more as a pious duty than a public trust. In the exercise of this duty, they were moreover in a position to safeguard the interests of their relatives in the clans which were the basic unit of the patriciate which ruled the towns. 'Charity begins at home' is also a Dutch proverb, although couched in the somewhat obscure expression 'The shirt (that is one's own) is closer (to the body) than the robe (of public office).'

If the ecclesiastical authorities of the new church were a dead loss to the artists of Holland, not so the laymen who ran institutions of welfare. They understood how to use art for public purposes, and were not averse to doing so. They did have to be careful, though. One of the charges of the iconoclasts – and of many more moderate Christians as well – was that the Catholic Church spent too much money on art and did not give enough to the poor. Once a slogan of that kind proves its effectiveness, it remains potent for a long time. The Protestants who were now entrusted with the funds for relief had to avoid

This part of Christianity was fortunately free from sectarianism. Van den Valckert worked for Catholics, de Bray for Calvinists and Verkolje for Mennonites.

This analysis does not begin to do justice to the rich imagery of our painting. However, it is unlikely that we will be able to decipher the painting satisfactorily until we find out more about the sitters and their ties to the painter.

Houbraken, vol. 1, p. 215. Van Thiel 1983, pp. 133, 182-183.

incurring the same charges that they themselves, in many cases, had hurled at their predecessors.

Within limits, however, there was a place of honour for art in the Dutch world of charity. In a recent dissertation, the American art historian Sheila Muller studied this phenomenon.[1] She distinguishes between three main types of art ordered by charitable bodies: sculptural decorations of the facades of institutions; group portraits of regents; and paintings symbolizing and glorifying their work.

The first new institutions to open under the Republic were the Amsterdam houses of correction for men and women, in 1596. They were extremely progressive for their time, if only because they served to punish criminals, beggars and such by incarceration and heavy labour rather than by branding, maiming or exile. The initiative behind the new establishments was taken by friends and followers of the biblical humanist Dirck Volckertsz. Coornhert, an avowed enemy of the Calvinists, and an outstanding engraver. Since the houses of correction were intended to be financially self-sufficient (they sold the labour of the inmates, charged admission to visitors and enjoyed certain trade advantages from the city and the province), they were freer than other institutions to indulge a taste for art. They ordered reliefs for their impressive entrance gates, were among the first group of charity regents to have their portrait painted, and attracted artists of all kinds to draw and engrave the goings-on within.

If Dutch charity began at home, it extended, in the first place, only as far as the parish borders. The highest ideal was also a practical one: to care adequately for one's own. Under the church, only parishioners were helped, and under the burgher regents, only registered citizens of the towns. Some of the charities were even stricter than that, operating more like retirement homes for paying customers than as welfare institutions. At the beginning of the Republic, the biblical humanists who designed the new institutions of charity believed that it was possible to defeat poverty by helping the deserving poor, coercing the undeserving into looking for gainful employ, and closing the town gates to undesirables from abroad. This proved to be an illusion. The prosperity of the Dutch cities attracted tens of thousands of immigrants from all over northern Europe, and not all of them were able to find work or support themselves. The streets of the towns began filling up with beggars whose presence undermined the confidence of the charitable rich that things were under control. To simply outlaw begging, as Amsterdam did in 1613, was obviously a hollow gesture. What may have helped would have been to redefine poverty in broader terms, and to create appropriately large-scale institutions to deal with it. But seventeenth-century Amsterdam was not fitted for that task. Instead, the existing institutions were beefed up, and the overflow from their work was picked up, with restrictions and limitations of all kinds, by the municipal College of Almoners.

One effect of the new measures was to add responsibility and prestige to the boards of the burgher charities. It was at this juncture that a new artistic tradition was born: the group portrait of charity regents. In 1617 and 1618, the first three such paintings came into being: the regents of the Amsterdam male house of detention, those of St. Peter's Hospital and of the home for the aged (fig. 4) were all painted by Cornelis van der Voort. The sitters had themselves

Fig. 4
CORNELIS VAN DER VOORT
*Regents of the home for the aged*, 1618. Canvas, 152 × 200 cm. Amsterdam, Amsterdams Historisch Museum.

shown sitting and standing at their work table; around them were deeds, documents and account books referring to their administrative responsibilities. The painter, an immigrant from Flanders, had – it is nearly redundant to say it – excellent contacts in Amsterdam. His brother was a wealthy landowner, and he himself was one of the leading art dealers in the city, with the portraits of several important persons and groups to his credit.

New traditions are born from old ones. For a century or more, Amsterdam civic bodies had been painted for the meeting halls where they assembled. But until 1617 only the officers and members of certain guilds and civic guard groups had been portrayed in this way, not the boards of institutions. Following the example set in 1617-18, many other boards of regents ordered group portraits in the decades to come. The practice remained limited, however, to Amsterdam and Haarlem.

In 1626, the Amsterdam Almoners also decided to have themselves painted

**28**

JAN VAN BIJLERT (1597–1671)
*Inmates of St. Job's Hospital, Utrecht, soliciting donations.*
Signed *J v Bijlert fecit.*
Canvas, 76.3 × 115.3 cm.

Utrecht, Centraal Museum, cat.nr. 57. Purchased in 1934 from Mrs. J. Vuyk, after the painting turned up in the American art trade in 1931.

The hospital of St. Job in Utrecht, as Marten Jan Bok has shown, was unique in its various connections with the world of art. The painter of this group portrait, Jan van Bijlert, joined the hospital board in 1634, but even before that the board room was decorated with a choice selection of work by painters from Utrecht and the surroundings. (Including Paulus Bor; see nr. 21).

As Bok has pointed out, this painting is the only known Dutch group portrait to depict poor people as the main figures. The exception reminds us with force of the truth that painted portraits are expensive luxuries which can only be afforded by people with money to spare.

Bok 1984.

**29**

JAN DE BRAY (ca. 1627–
1697)
*Admitting children to the
Haarlem church orphanage.*
Signed and dated *JDBray
1663*. Canvas, 134.5 × 154
cm.

Haarlem, Frans Hals-
museum, cat. nr. 35.

See text.

Fig. 5

WERNER VAN DEN
VALCKERT (attributed)
*An almoner and chief provost
of the Amsterdam College of
Almoners visiting a poor
family*, 1626 or 1627.
Panel, 149 × 151.5 cm.
Amsterdam, Amsterdams
Historisch Museum.

(fig. 5). They were the closest approximation in the city to a public welfare department, and apparently they did not think it appropriate to have themselves shown within the closed space of an office, like the regents of the more parochial charities. In five paintings, we see them engaged in their day-to-day work: registering new recipients of charity, distributing bread and clothing, looking in on the hennep works which they ran, and visiting the house of a poor family. In contrast to the group portraits of regents, the depiction of charity as it was actually practiced did not become a recognized category in Dutch painting.

The duty to help one's fellow man in need was, in the seventeenth century, considered a religious one. Those who practiced it looked forward to the moment described in Matthew 25: 'When the Son of man comes in his glory, ...he will say to those at his right hand, "Come, O blessed of my Father, inherit the kingdom prepared for you from the foundation of the world; for I was hungry and you gave me food; I was thirsty and you gave me drink, I was a stranger and you welcomed me, I was naked and you clothed me, I was sick and you visited me, I was in prison and you came to me."' The faithful ask the Lord in surprise when they performed these acts, and he replies: 'Truly, I say to you, as you did it to one of the least of these my brethren, you did it to me.' To these acts of kindness to the living, Christian tradition later added the burial of the dead, as the last of the Seven Works of Mercy.

Although Dutch charity put more emphasis on helping the *brethren*, in the limited sense of fellow citizens or parishioners, than the parable of the talents may have intended, the regents of institutions nonetheless thought of themselves as being at the right hand of Christ. Complementing the portraits of themselves at their voluntary service, they also hung in their board rooms paintings of the Seven Works of Mercy, which revealed the greater goodness of their work. Depictions of all the works of mercy in one canvas are easy to recognize; but acts of mercy could also be tucked away into a landscape, a scene from everday life or a biblical subject. A painting of that sort, encountered on the wall of a charitable institution, would be perceived as a depiction of charity. But once it is removed from its original site and cast onto the art market or hung in a museum, it becomes a mere landscape or genre painting or history painting, incapable of arousing the same emotions as in its original location.

One of the most original paintings ever made for a Dutch charity is that painted by Jan de Bray in 1663 for the Haarlem orphanage (cat.nr.29). The burghers working in the institution are shown as figures in a living parable, feeding the hungry and clothing the naked before our eyes. What makes the scene all the more unusual is that a Calvinist minister stands beside the woman volunteer, who looks towards heaven as she does her work. The church tower in the left background adds to the ecclesiastical flavour of the scene. In fact, the Haarlem orphanage was exceptional in that it *was* run by the Calvinist church. De Bray's painting shows us what charity looked like through Calvinist eyes: a purely religious act, to be performed with one's gaze directed at God and a minister at one's elbow. What a contrast it forms with the depiction of the Amsterdam almoners, which, even though it contains some symbolic references to the divine inspiration behind charity, is a picture of civic, if moral, virtue. If we think of charity as a significant indicator of the way people think about and act towards each other, we recognize in these two fascinating works a fundamental dichotomy in Dutch life, between the humanist tradition and the Calvinist one.

An appeal to heaven is also made by one of the figures in the only known group portrait of the *inmates* of a Dutch institution. The third figure from the left in Jan van Bijlert's *Inmates of St. Job's Hospital soliciting donations* (cat.nr.28) raises a finger to the sky while addressing the man next to him, who is holding a collecting box. This unprecedented and unimitated work shows some of the nineteen old men who lived at St. Job's, dressed in their institutional white doublets. (The outpatients were syphilitics – St. Job's was the first hospital in the

Naamen der Regenten
van het
St: Joris Proveniers-huijs:
Beginnende met deszelfs aanvang.
Op den 10de. Januarij des Jaars 1707.
PIETER REIJNST
ANDRIES PATIJN

**30**

ANONYMOUS
1700s

Names of the regents of
the St. Joris Proveniershuis.

Haarlem, Frans Hals-
museum. Panel, 165 × 135
cm.

Board membership on a
charitable institution was,
and often still is, as much a
social distinction as a pious
duty. Not all boards had
themselves immortalized
in group portraits, but
even those that did would
also have their names
painted on boards of this
kind, which today are
rarer than painted por-
traits.

   The inmates of the
Haarlem Proveniershuis
were not the poorest
people in the city. They
were registered citizens,
and paid for the right to
spend their old age in what
were very comfortable and
charming surroundings.

country for syphilis patients.) Only the two men on the right – the housemaster
and beadle – are dressed as burghers. The regents who ordered the painting left
themselves out of it altogether.

   Recent research by the Utrecht historian Marten Jan Bok suggests a reason
why the regents of St. Job's may have chosen to hang up this remarkable
composition.[2] Until 1634, the institution enjoyed the privilege of conducting
two annual collections: they would send the old men from the home out to
bring in money to pay for the care of the outpatients. However, this form of
legalized begging was being eliminated all through the country, and in August
1634 the Utrecht city council annulled the historical right of St. Job's to the
two annual drives. The regents protested mightily, and in the end, after May
1635, were able to negotiate a settlement in the form of financial compensation.
If van Bijlert's painting was made in the course of the struggle (the stylistic
evidence does not rule out the possibility), it can be seen as a painted plea on the
part of the regents: how can you refuse these poor old men the pittance they
ask of you for the sake of their suffering fellows? Do they call in vain on God,
and on you?

   One of those regents was, from November 1634 on, the painter himself. It
took the coincidence of a talented and original painter being on the board of a
charitable institution to make possible the creation of this completely
unconventional work. And even then, the painter would need the sympathetic
collusion of his colleagues. But that was less of a problem in St. Job's than
anywhere else: among the regents there must have been more art lovers than
only Jan van Bijlert. Between 1622 and 1642, the institution served as a kind of
showroom for the work of Utrecht artists, before they had a permanent
exhibition space of their own. In that period thirty-five Utrecht painters gave
examples of their work to the hospital, which kept them until the early
nineteenth century. Seven of the specialists in history painting (among them
van Bijlert, in 1628) chose subjects from the book of Job, but the majority of
the paintings had nothing at all to do with the hospital. There were still-lifes of
fruit, fish and fowl, landscapes with and without animals, ruins and mountains,
genre paintings, heads, and a *Sleeping Venus*. (Although the latter may be less
inappropriate than it seems, in view of the medical specialty of St. Job's.)

   The Utrecht hospital of St. Job stood alone in Holland as the recipient of a
small collection of paintings by local masters. But even in the absence of such
exceptional circumstances, the board room of many a Dutch institution of
charity echoed with discussions of the merits of paintings, the morality of
spending money on them, and the political expediency of displaying them. We
are no longer surprised that an English visitor to the Netherlands in 1688,
William Carr, commenting on the Dutch love of pictures, should have noted in
passing that even the alms-houses were 'richly adorned' with them.[3] Two

hundred years later, the same could no longer be said. There was hardly an institution in the country which could afford to hold on to its valuables, or cared to. The fate of the collection of St.Job's, this time, is unfortunately typical rather than exceptional: in 1811 the paintings they had received from the painters of Utrecht were sold at auction for sixty-two guilders.

1. Muller 1985. Much of the information for the present chapter was derived from this very interesting book, which is a revised version of a dissertation for the Univesity of California, Berkeley, 1982.
2. Bok 1984.
3. Quoted in Boxer 1965, p.171, from W. Carr, *A description of Holland*, ed. 1691, p.27.

# Craft and commerce

'For witt, they seeme a very simple people,... but howsoever they seeme, no doubt the men are indeede most Crafty espetially in traffique, eating up all nations therein, by frugallity, industry, and subtilety,... and are indeede most witty in all meanes to grow rich, as the experience of our age hath taught us.'[1]

Another stereotype, like that of the disapproving Dutch Calvinists. But this one is harder to discredit. It was written by an Englishman, Fynes Morrison, in 1614, and the 'experience' he mentioned was all too real. 'In 1606,' notes the historian of Amsterdam capitalism Violet Barbour, 'a member of the House of Commons maintained that the Dutch could sell English cloth dressed in the Netherlands and re-exported thence, more cheaply than the English trading companies could do.'[2] And Barbour says he was right. Today, not even the most vociferous opponent of Japanese underselling in the United States Senate could cite trade exploits as stunning as that.

The secret of this particular kind of success is the wit, if you want to call it that, to offer better credit terms and lower interest to your suppliers and customers than anyone else. The banks and traders of Amsterdam could do that, in the sixteenth and seventeenth centuries, because they had more capital than they needed for their own businesses, or than they could invest at a good return in their own country. How they accumulated this capital is actually not a very pretty story. It came largely from the enormous profits that they made selling Baltic grain to the Mediterranean during a lengthy drought. As the only merchant shipping power in the world capable of handling the immense volumes involved, the Dutch could dictate favourable terms both to the seller and the buyer, and they did. Their position was enhanced by some concurrent military developments: the Spanish armada was defeated, half of the Antwerp business establishment fled to Amsterdam, and the half that stayed behind was paralyzed by a Dutch blockade.

Not all capital was plowed frugally back into business. Most merchants and traders liked to keep enough of it at home in order to build comfortable houses and buy nice things, like paintings. The Baltic traders were good customers, van Mander tells us, for portraits. But so were many others. For this section of the exhibition we are in search of paintings that take trade itself as their subject or paintings of merchants in their mercantile capacity. And these we do not find in the grain trade. People in that line of business tend to keep a low profile. A merchant who cornered wheat in Gdansk in expectation of a poor harvest in

the Po valley was not likely to hang up paintings divulging the size and
whereabouts of his silos. If he did wish to glorify his work in art, he might have
done so symbolically, for example with a painting of the biblical hero Joseph
distributing grain to the Egyptians when their seven fat years were followed by
seven lean ones. When the wealthiest of the Dutch traders in the Baltic, the
Trips, commissioned paintings commemorating their operations in northern
Europe, it was not their speculation in the staff of life that they depicted, but
their role as merchants of death: arms manufacture, at a well-guarded plant
protected by Swedish guarantees. Allaert van Everdingen painted vistas of their
plant, while their house in Amsterdam was adorned with sculptures of cannon.[3]

One of the branches of business that did turn to art to advertise itself was, as
Linda Stone has shown in a fascinating study, the textile trade.[4] In contrast to
grain and shipping, which were dominated by the Dutch, textile was a highly
competitive international industry. This is well illustrated by the above
quotation from the Parliamentary speech of 1606: Dutch merchants bought
*English* cloth to sell to the English, rather than the product they could have
bought in Holland.

The main textile product of Holland in the first decade of the seventeenth
century was Leiden say, a light wool manufactured by the 'new drapery,'
which had eclipsed the traditional heavy Leiden woolens. The growing market
for say was a function of changing fashion and price competition, but the rise of
Leiden as a manufacturing centre was a planned move that took place
overnight. When the Spanish made life impossible for the Protestant say
workers of the Flemish city of Hondschoote, the town council of Leiden passed
a special ordinance, in December 1582, to facilitate their resettlement in their
city. Within two years, say accounted for eight out of ten bolts of cloth
produced in Leiden.

At the beginning of the seventeenth century, the guild of the say drapers was
the only textile guild in Leiden with a building of its own. For that guildhall,
between 1594 and 1612, a series of six large paintings was made by Isaac Claesz.
van Swanenburgh depicting and allegorizing the industry and its place in
Leiden. In 1602, the artist was commissioned by the town government (of
which he was an important member) to design eleven stained-glass panels with
the same theme, as a tribute to the legendary city father Jan van Hout, 'who
was largely responsible for encouraging the large influx of Flemish and Brabant
émigrés to Leiden.'[5] These works were as unprecedented in their composition
as in their conception, and one cannot help wondering to what extent their
existence and originality were due to Isaac Claesz.'s ability to influence events
in the town council.

One painting in the series combines four distinct operations – the spinning,

**31**
FRANS HALS (1580/85–1666)
*Portrait of a man.* Painted about 1635. Canvas, 121 × 90 cm. (after restoration in 1985–1986).

Rotterdam, Museum Boymans-van Beuningen, inv.nr. 1276. Acquired in 1865, after having been sold at auction three times in the preceding twenty years.

Slive 1974, p. 59, nr. 106.

reeling, warping and weaving of the wool – in a single scene (fig.2). The well-dressed workers perform their job in a bright, airy space looking out onto the Oosterlingplaats in Leiden, the square where the cloth market for 'Easterners,' i.e. Baltic merchants, was held. As Stone points out, this idealized vision of saymaking is a far cry from the reality. The town of Leiden was quick enough to bring the Flemings to their city, but once they had been registered as citizens and guild members and put to work, the town showed itself unwilling to invest in decent living and work accomodations for them. Only when the workers threatened desertion did the town come across, in 1596, by converting an old convent into 'sixty-three small weavers' homes measuring only 6.91 by 3.53 meters each. A home comprised two rooms: one for the loom, and one for cooking and sleeping.'[6] Van Swanenburgh's paintings, then, for all their technical accuracy and suggested realism, are not so much pictures of Leiden labourers at their work as evocations of an employer's dream.

The ascendancy of the new drapery in Leiden did not last long. By 1620 the production of say peaked, and in the decades to come it lost ground dramatically to its old rival, pure wool cloth. In part, this was a case of big fish eating little ones. The production of wool cloth demanded more capital than the new drapery, and the heavy investors it attracted found it relatively easy, in a period of decline, to buy out the smaller operators in say and put them to work as supervisors in their own much larger businesses. Their guild put up its hall, the Lakenhal, in the 1630s. In 1648, the founding year of the Leiden painters' guild, the township voted to give the Lakenhal two hundred guilders a year to order paintings and other artistic adornments for the building, which today is the town museum.

The first such commission was for three allegorical paintings of Leiden and the drapery trade (cat.nr.32). The artist chosen for the honour was Abraham van den Tempel, who was a cloth merchant himself, and one of the founding members of the painters' guild. In 1652 he was paid a thousand guilders for the series, painted in 1650 and 1651. The painting in the exhibition shows the maid of Leiden welcoming an allegorical figure of the Cloth Trade. Freedom kneels before the throne of Leiden, while Minerva the goddess of wisdom (and the emblem of Leiden University) and Mercury the god of trade look on approvingly. The painting and its two companions breathe the spirit of '48, the year of the triumphant Peace of Münster, ending the Eighty Years War. The country resounded with rhetoric that was music to the ears of the Leiden wool merchants. The grandiloquence of van den Tempel's series has no measurable distance at all to the work even of the bosses.

In Haarlem, where the textile industry had a different structure, we find it

**32**

ABRAHAM VAN DEN
TEMPEL (1622/23-1672)
*The maid of Leiden receiving
the maid of the cloth trade.*
Signed and dated *AB van d
Tempel f A 1651.* Canvas,
207 × 266.5 cm.

Leiden, Stedelijk Museum
De Lakenhal, inv.nr. 427.
Painted as one of a series of
three allegories for the
Governors' Room of the
Lakenhal when it was still
the headquarters of the
Leiden woolen industry.

For the artist's connection
with his subject, see the
text. Van den Tempel's
allegories are a case study
in the relativity of taste. In
1750, they were admired
vastly by Jan van Gool, the
author of a book of lives
of the Dutch artists, but by
1794 they were said to be
inferior to the artist's
portraits, and in the
twentieth century they
were singled out for dis-
praise by Abraham Bre-
dius and Willem Martin.
In 1981 the present painting was included in the
major exhibition *Gods,*

*saints and heroes,* a turning
point in the revaluation of
historical and allegorical
painting in the seventeenth
century in Holland.

Wijnman 1959, p. 64. A.
Blankert, in exhib. cat.
*God en de goden,* nr. 53.

**33**

CORNELIS DECKER
(before 1625–1678)
*A weaver's workshop.*
Signed and dated *C.Decker
1659*. Panel, 45 × 57 cm.

Amsterdam, Rijks-
museum, inv.nr. A 2562.
Presented by the estate of
C. Hoogendijk, 1912.

See text.

**34**

JOB ADRIAENSZ.
BERCKHEYDE (1630-1693)
*The courtyard of the
Amsterdam stock exchange,
after 1668*. Signed *Job
Berckheyde*. Canvas,
89 × 116 cm.

Amsterdam, Amsterdams
Historisch Museum,
cat.nr. 47, inv.nr. A 3025.
Acquired with the col-
lection bequeathed to the
city of Amsterdam by
Adriaan van der Hoop
(1778-1854), which be-
came municipal property
only after the death dues

had been paid by a group
of private individuals.

The Amsterdam stock
exchange, built to the
plans of the Amsterdam
city architect Hendrick de
Keyser in 1608-1611, was a
symbol in the seventeenth
century for world trade, as
Wall Street is today.
The building itself was
based on the design of the
London stock exchange,
and was not very original.
What made it so famous
was the sheer volume and
geographical extent of the
dealing.

The statue of Mercury,
the god of trade, in the
upper left, was added to
the building when the
southern facade was rebuilt
in 1668. Berckheyde
painted the building at
least two more times.

depicted in another kind of art. Instead of the highly centralized woolen trade of Leiden, Haarlem had a linen industry with a form of its own. There were weavers – once again Flemish immigrants – who owned one or two looms which they operated themselves. The flax cloth they wove – world-famous, especially in the costly variety of damast – was then laid out to bleach in fields on the outskirts of the city belonging to wealthy landowners. The paintings of the Haarlem textile industry show both kinds of work: the weavers in their ateliers (cat. nr. 33), and the bleaching fields (fig. 6), both equally picturesque.

Fig. 6
JACOB VAN RUISDAEL
*Bleaching fields outside Haarlem, seen from the dunes at Overveen.* After 1660. Canvas, 55.5 × 62 cm. The Hague, Mauritshuis.

The paintings of Haarlem textile manufacture are more down to earth than those of Leiden, and seem to be more purely descriptive. But they too idealize existing conditions and serve commercial purposes. The small weavers of Haarlem were actually so dissatisfied with their livelihoods that many of them sold their looms eagerly in order to speculate in tulip bulbs, during the great boom of 1636. The crash of 1637 left many of them penniless, and forced them to begin weaving again as hired hands or junior partners. The image of the independent craftsman whose time is his own, as in Cornelis Decker's painting, was a flattered one. And so were Jacob van Ruisdael's views of the bleaching fields. He always shows the most expensive fields, those closest to the city, with the Haarlem skyline serving as a kind of visual tradename for the product in the foreground. (Decker, by the way, also made forest landscapes in the style of Jacob van Ruisdael. They must have had the same customers.) There was a brief flourishing of Haarlem textile paintings in the mid-seventeenth century, with dozens of local masters producing very similar subjects, and then it was over. One is hard put to name another group of Dutch paintings of trade and commerce showing such a concentration of time, place and motif. Not even in nearby Amsterdam, where the thousands who lived from the textile trade included many art lovers, do we find an equivalent.

The works we have discussed are exceptional in that they betray the existence of formal business organizations with an interest in the creation of paintings of particular kinds. The more general ties between art and trade are so vast and so pervasive that we could not begin to illustrate them here. Suffice it to say that even if one does not want to think of artists as commercial traders when they sell their work, the painters of Holland were still participants in the world of commerce. Most of them, in the sixteenth and seventeenth centuries at least, had sources of income aside from their art, in activities which may not be all that far removed from their work as artists. Such as trading in real estate, like the landscape painter Jan van Goyen, or running a brewery, like the painter of good drunken fun Jan Steen, or skippering, like Barend Cornelisz. Kleenknecht, specialist in seascapes. With these few examples, I wish to suggest that motives of a commercial nature sometimes played a role in a painter's choice of specialty. Such connections, I know from personal experience, can sometimes bring the art of the past closer than any amount of aestheticizing 'art appreciation.'

If painters could be business-like, patrons and collectors could be sentimental. In 1814, the Amsterdam banker Adriaan van der Hoop was on the welcoming committee when the Tsar of Russia, Alexander I, honoured the venerable stock exchange with a visit. Twenty-two years later, when that landmark of seventeenth-century civic architecture was about to be demolished, van der Hoop paid the young Kaspar Karsen seven hundred guilders to paint the courtyard of the building, from a point of view which showed the plaque commemorating the Tsar's visit (cat.nr. 36). That van der Hoop, of all those who had worked in the stock exchange, thought of having it immortalized in this way had to do with the fact that he had since become one of the foremost art collectors in the city. This gave him the impulse and a second, special reason to want to own a painting of the old exchange. Since 1822, the Academy of Drawing (where Karsen himself had been trained) was located in the upper story of the building.

That which the nineteenth century commemorated in its decline was celebrated by the seventeenth in its rise. When the stock exchange was sixty years old, in 1668, it was expanded on the south. The new situation was

## 35

BARTHOLOMEUS VAN
DER HELST (1613-1670)
*The Amsterdam merchant
Daniel Bernard (1626-1714).*
Signed and dated
*Bartholomeus vander helst.
1669.* One of the letters on
the table is addressed to M.
Neufville and signed by
A. Bernard, another to
Pauwels Sloot, signed by
D. Bernard and dated
June 8, 1669. The books
on the shelf are marked
*Venditie...* (Sales) and
*Factuurboeck van incomend...
beginnende 12 December*
(Invoices received).
Canvas, 124 × 113 cm.

Rotterdam, Museum
Boymans-van Beuningen,
inv.nr. 1297. Purchased in
1865 at sale Baron van
Brienen van de Groot
Lindt, Paris, May 8, 1865,
for 500 guilders. The sitter
was not an ancestor of the
Baron, who was from a
family of wealthy Catholic
merchants. A painting of
this description was sold at
auction in Amsterdam on
26 July 1775 for one hun-
dred guilders to the art
dealer Yver.

In 1669, the forty-three
year old Daniel Bernard
was a partner in a firm still
run by his father and
uncle, trading with Rus-
sia, Spain, Italy and the
Middle East. The main
asset of the house was a
charter from the Tsar,
acquired with the help of
Stadholder Frederik Hen-
drik in 1628. Daniel was

to continue running it, at
great profit, for the rest of
his life. In the years after
this portrait was painted,
he occupied various posi-
tions in the town govern-
ment and its trading
companies, rising to the
dignity of alderman in 1681.

The tower in the back-
ground most closely re-
sembles the Jan Rooden-
poorttoren on the Singel,
not far from Bernard's
house on the Keizersgracht
near the Leliegracht.

De Gelder 1921, cat.nr. 50.

**36**

KASPAR KARSEN (1810–1896)
*The Amsterdam stock exchange before its demolition in 1837.* Signed and dated *K. Karssen 1836.* Canvas, 87 × 109 cm.

Amsterdam, Amsterdams Historisch Museum, inv.nr.s 7526. From the van der Hoop collection; for provenance, see above, cat.nr. 34.

The banker Adriaan van der Hoop began to collect seriously only in 1832. His main interest was in Dutch painting of the seventeenth century, but he also gave commissions to living artists (see also cat.nr. 55). In this case, the commission was partly inspired by his purchase in 1833 of a painting of the old stock exchange by Job Berck-heyde (cat.nr. 34). For the collector's personal memories of the building, see the text.

De Bruyn Kops 1964.

recorded by Job Berckheyde (cat.nr.34), perhaps for some Amsterdam banker of his own time. Or was it a textile merchant? From 1660 through the mid-eighteenth century, the city salesroom for woolen cloth was housed in the upper story of the stock exchange.

As a collector of paintings, van der Hoop was able to enjoy the best of both worlds: he owned Berckheyde's view of the stock exchange as well as Karsen's. In the normal course of events, the two paintings, which gain so much when we see them through the eyes of van der Hoop, would have been dispersed on the market to end up in different collections, as haphazard examples of 'topographical art.' However, van der Hoop bequeathed his collection as a whole to the city of Amsterdam, which has found a place for these two paintings in the Amsterdam Historical Museum. In that endlessly fascinating presentation, they serve a function at least as rich as they once did on the walls of Adriaan van der Hoop's cabinet.

1. Jacobsen Jensen 1918, p.288.
2. Barbour 1950, p.95.
3. Meischke and Reeser 1983.
4. Stone-Ferrier 1985, from which I have derived much of the material for this section of the catalogue.
5. Stone-Ferrier, p.2.
6. Stone-Ferrier, pp.28-29.

# Deeds of glory, acts of God

When Jan Vos wished to recommend the art of painting to the burgomasters of Amsterdam for their patronage, he did not tell them how beautiful their new town hall would be with pictures on the walls. Instead, he reminded them in an epic poem entitled *The Struggle of Nature and Death, or The Triumph of Painting* of the mortality of human flesh and the longevity of art: *ars longa, vita brevis*. If they wanted to be remembered after they were gone, they should have themselves and their deeds recorded in paint. For millennia, this simple truth, conveyed persuasively to susceptible ears, has helped artists tap one of their largest sources of income.

In the art of painting, the urge for immortality benefitted two kinds of specialty in particular: portraiture, of course, and history painting. Preserving a record of one's personal appearance, perhaps dignified with uniform, signs of honour or office, house and family, has seemed to many people worth the price of a portrait. Whether the Dutch take the record for portraits per capita I do not know, but they are certainly a contender.

While a portrait may include attributes referring to particular moments in a person's life, it was not customary to dedicate entire paintings to such events. Pictures of weddings, private celebrations, triumphs in business or career, are as good as unknown in Holland. In that area the painter came far behind the silversmith, who would often be called upon to make inscribed beakers or plates commemorating landmarks in the lives of private people.

Not that painters were shut out altogether from this area of the market: a newly-wed couple, or the father of a bride, may have commissioned or received as a gift a painting of the wedding of Alexander the Great and Roxane, or the meeting of Isaac and Rebecca; a grand banquet may have been commemorated with the purchase of a painting of the feast of the gods; a merchant who made a fortune in spices from the east may have hung a painting of Jupiter bringing the Asian princess Europa to the west. By doing so, they would be taking advantage of a code that allowed people to flaunt their best moments without seeming vain.

Even civic and national events, commemorated in paint as well as in silver, were seldom depicted directly. They too were subsumed under time-honoured prototypes. The paintings that the burgomasters of Amsterdam finally did order for the town hall, for example, evoked the Dutch revolt against Spain in the form of scenes from Tacitus's description of the revolt of the Batavians

## 37

EVERT CRIJNSZ. VAN DER
MAES (1577–1656)
*Ensign of the Orange
Company of the St. Sebas-
tian civic guard, The Hague.*
Signed and dated 1617.
Canvas, 200 × 103 cm.

The Hague, Gemeente-
museum, inv. nr. 314.
(Under nr. 227, the
museum holds a painting
of another ensign of the St.
Sebastian civic guard, with
nearly the same
dimensions, and a very
similar, symmetrical
composition. That work is
signed by Joachim Ottensz.
Houckgeest and dated
1621.)

In The Hague there were
two civic guards: the old,
aristocratic St. George
Guards, and the bourgeois
St. Sebastian Guards. This
unidentified ensign was
attached to one of the four
companies of the St. Se-
bastian Guards. The offi-
cers of the guards – cap-
tains, lieutenants and en-
signs – were usually men
of some importance in the
civic and business life of
the town.
    The painter Evert
Crijnsz. van der Maes
came from the same circles
as his sitter. His brother
Seger Crijnsz. van der
Maes was captain of one of
the other companies of St.
Sebastian from 1614 to
1620, and in the year of
this portrait became an
alderman of The Hague.
Seger himself was a painter

of stained-glass windows – and of banners! The van der Maeses shared their prominence in the world of official Hague painting with the van Ravesteyns. In 1616, for example, Jan Anthonisz. van Ravesteyn (ca. 1572-1657) painted the officers of the Orange company on the steps of the town hall after being received by the burgo-masters, and in 1618 im-mortalized a reception of the combined St. Sebastian Guards, of which he was one, for the burgomasters. In the preceding genera-tion, the fathers of van der Maes and Ravesteyn had collaborated on stained-glass commissions for The Hague in 1593 and 1602. We are in the presence of what one might call a military-artistic complex, of a kind one also en-counters in Amsterdam in the same years.

For Seger Crijnsz. van der Maes and Ravesteyn, see Martin 1923-24, Bredius and Moes 1881.

against Rome. Even the idea to do so was derived from an earlier example. In 1612, Otto van Veen painted a series of such scenes which were sold to the States General by his brother Pieter, who held a high government position. To us, this indirectness may seem like evasiveness, a flight from facts into phrases. But to poets, painters and audiences of the time the parallels between present and past added resonance to the events of their own day.

There were exceptions to this rule. Some contemporary occurrences did merit undisguised representation on their own. Sieges and battles were often painted in a repertorial mode. The lifting of the siege of Leiden in 1574 became a popular motif (fig. 7). Famous disasters and natural prodigies too were immortalized with a nearly documentary precision, as were unique events of state: the signing and celebration of the Treaty of Münster, the arrivals and departures of deposed rulers. Between them these few categories account for nearly all non-allegorical Dutch paintings of contemporary events.

One can try to look for a principle underlying these exceptions. Perhaps certain events appealed so strongly to the imagination that viewers insisted on authentic particulars rather than rhetorical commentary on the higher significance of things. Or could it be that the death in battles and disasters of people one knew seemed to demand more direct commemoration than was possible within the prevailing conventions? Perhaps questions of that kind will someday be answerable in such terms, if the 'history of mentalities' is ever applied with sufficient insight to the Dutch Republic. In the meanwhile, we have to be content with more prosaic suggestions.

Fig. 7
OTTO VAN VEEN
*Distributing bread and herring in Leiden, 1574.*
Panel, 40 × 59.5 cm.
Amsterdam,
Rijksmuseum.

**38**

ADAM WILLAERTS (1577-1664)
*The departure of Frederick V, elector of the Palatinate, from England to Vlissingen, 1613(?)*. Signed and dated *A. Willaerts 1619*. Canvas, 88 × 142 cm.

The Netherlands Office for Fine Arts, inv.nr.NK 2368 (on loan to Nederlands Scheepvaartmuseum, Amsterdam).

1619 was a great year in the life of Frederick V. Elected king of Bohemia by the Protestant nobility in August, he entered Prague in October and was crowned in November.

His only better year was 1613, when he sailed to England from Holland to marry the daughter of King James I, Elizabeth Stuart, in a magnificent celebration for which Shakespeare wrote *King Henry VIII*.

Frederick was the nephew of the Dutch stadholder Maurits and his brother Frederik Hendrik, who came over for the occasion. His connection with the house of Orange and his popularity among the Dutch were a great good fortune to him when, in 1620, he lost his throne, and had to flee to Holland. There, as the 'Winter King,' he kept a rich court in exile for the rest of his life.

Adam Willaerts, who had lived in England himself for some time before his marriage in 1605, was one of the Dutch painters to be patronized by the Winter King. Above the mantlepiece in one of the rooms of Frederick's country home in Rhenen hung a painting by Willaerts – perhaps this one, for all we know. The representation is a bit puzzling, and may be a composite of more than one occurrence in the life of its hero. It has been suggested that the castle in the background is the Hradschin in Prague, which became Frederick's in 1619. The late date in itself cannot be an objection to the identification of the subject. In 1623 the town of Haarlem commissioned a painting of the arrival of Frederick V in Vlissingen from Hendrick Vroom.

Van Luttervelt 1947. Bol 1973. Bok 1984, pp. 102-104.

90

**39**

EGBERT VAN DER POEL
(1621-1664)

*The explosion of the powder magazine in Delft, 1654.* Signed *E. van der Poel* and inscribed *12 oct 1654*. Panel, 32 × 39 cm.

The Netherlands Office for Fine Arts, inv.nr. NK 2784. Confiscated by the Germans from the D. Hoogendijk gallery, Amsterdam. During the war it was in Hitler's collection.

'A large part of Delft was destroyed by the explosion of a powder magazine on the morning of Monday, 12 October 1654, at 10.30 a.m. This magazine lay in the North-East corner of the town, near to the Geerweg. According to the account given by Dirck van Bleyswijck, at the time of the explosion the magazine contained between 80,000 and 90,000 pounds of powder, and the force of the explosion was so great that it completely destroyed all the houses in the area bounded on the North by the the Geerweg, on the West by the Verwersdijk, on the South by the Doelenstraat and on the East by the Singel canal; many houses beyond were wrecked and there was lesser damage throughout Delft. Of the magazine itself nothing was left and on its site was a deep pool full of water (presumably the one visible towards the right in the picture). The number of those killed was never known; among them was Carel Fabritius, who was taken out of the ruins dying.... The area of complete devastation was not rebuilt and served afterwards as a horse market, and much of it is an open space to this day.'

Painting the Delft explosion became a specialty in itself for van der Poel, who produced at least a dozen versions of this scene, and for several other Delft painters, including Daniel Vosmaer. This is a poignant fact in view of Vosmaer's collaboration with the most famous victim of the explosion, Carel Fabritius (see cat.nr. 87).

MacLaren 1960, from which it is always a pleasure to quote, p. 292, nr. 1061.

**40**

PIETER WOUWERMAN
(1623-1682)
*The recapture of Coevorden
by the States army, 30
December 1672.* Signed
*P.W.* Canvas, 65.5 × 80.5
cm.

Amsterdam, Rijks-
museum, inv.nr.A 486.
From the National
Museum, 1808.

The French invasion of the
Republic in June 1672
was the occasion of the
bloodiest fighting on

Dutch soil in a century.
While Louis XIV led his
troops into the country
from the south, his ally the
bishop of Münster came in
from the east. He laid siege
to Coevorden on July 1st,
and began a heavy bom-
bardment. After eleven
days, the garrison, en-
sconced in its 'impreg-
nable' fort, capitulated.
With the strongest point
in Drenthe under his
command, the bishop now
undertook an abortive
attack on Groningen.

One of those to leave

the captured city was the
Coevorden schoolmaster
Meyndert van Thienen. In
Groningen, he convinced
the commandant – a
German officer in the
service of the States
General – to try to retake
the city. During a cold
spell at the end of De-
cember, with the moats
frozen, a troop of 1500
men was able to recapture
Coevorden in an hour, and
then take its time to
plunder it. (In many parts
of the country, Dutch
property owners were

more afraid of the States
army, consisting largely of
ill-disciplined mercenaries,
than of the enemy.)

The ignominy of July
was forgotten and the
glory of December
immortalized in a day of
thanksgiving and a flood
of medals, prints and
paintings. The seven-sided
fortress proved to be more
effective in the hands of
artists than of soldiers.

Veenhoven 1969, pp.80-
89.

**41**

WILLEM VAN DE VELDE
THE YOUNGER (1633–
1707)
*Battle at sea*. Canvas,
85 × 110 cm.

The Netherlands Office for
Fine Arts, inv. nr. NK
2367 (on loan to Neder-
lands Scheepvaartmu-
seum). From the D. Katz
gallery, Dieren, and the
Silang collection, Amsterdam. During the war in
Hitler's collection.

Willem van de Velde the
younger was the son of a
prominent painter of sea-

scapes, who specialized in
black-and-white 'pen
paintings.' (They are
actually more like brush
drawings on the scale of
paintings.) The father of
the elder van de Velde was
a skipper and soldier, so
fighting and the sea were
in their blood.

Alfred von Wurzbach
remarked of our painter:
'A ship, to him, was as a
human sitter to a portraitist: an animate creature
with countless identifying
features and distinctions.'
His career began around
the time of the First
Anglo-Dutch War (1652–

1654), when he accompa-
nied his father aboard
admiralty men-o'-war to
immortalize engagements
at sea for the States General. In the naval battles of
the 1670s between the
Republic and England, the
van de Veldes were to be
found aboard British
vessels, in his majesty's service.

In our painting a Dutch
ship with the arms of
Haarlem on the stern is
engaged with a French
vessel flying a blue flag
with a madonna. On the
left, behind a burning
French man-o'-war, is the

Dutch flagship, identified
by the arms of Holland.
This would seem to indi-
cate a date in 1673, when
the Dutch were at war
with the French on land
and with the French and
English at sea. However,
by 1672 at the latest
Willem van de Velde the
Younger had moved to
London, which makes it
difficult to date the painting.

Wurzbach, vol. 2, pp. 755–
757. MacLaren 1960,
p. 420.

**42-51**

BERNARDUS ACCAMA
(1697–1756)
*Ten portraits of officers of the Oranje-Friesland Regiment, 1731: Colonel Watze Wytze van Cammingha and Captains Tulkens, Aylva van Hornhuisen, van Glinstra, Brunet, Haersma, Sloterdijk, Drevon, Haersolte and Alberti. Canvases, each ca. 97.5 × 75.5 cm.*

The paintings are from a numbered series of 24, of which the Fries Museum owns 23. Colonel van Cammingha, a scion of the same house that produced the sitter for cat.nr. 10, was colonel of the first battalion of the regiment.

Leeuwarden, Fries Museum.

CAMMINGA. COL: COM:

TULKENS Capt

ACILVA VAN HORNHUISEN Capt

N VAN GLINSTRA Capt

BRUNES Capt

H HAERSMA Capt

SLOTERDIJK Capt

DRE VON Capt

HAERSOLTE Capt

X GERTT Capt

**52**

ADRIAAN DE LELIE (1755-1820), the main figures, and EGBERT VAN DRIELST (1745-1818), the rest of the painting
*General Daendels taking leave in Maarssen of Lieutenant-Colonel C.R.T. Kraijenhoff, whom he was despatching to Amsterdam to help depose the city government, 18 January 1795.*
Signed and dated *E. van Drielst pinx. A. de Lelie A°₀ 1795.* On the back of the panel is a manuscript dated 1834 explaining the subject. Panel, 45 × 60 cm.

Amsterdam, Rijksmuseum, inv.nr. A 2231. Purchased in 1906 from the Nagel family, Arnhem.

Colonel Kraijenhoff was the military member of the Batavian Revolutionary Committee, a body of Patriots which was helping the French army to overthrow Stadholder Willem V in order to establish a Batavian Republic. After the French took Utrecht, Kraijenhoff was sent to Amsterdam on his own by the revolutionary general H.W. Daendels from

Maarssen, between Utrecht and Amsterdam. He arrived in the city in French uniform and demanded the resignation of the town council. Although the French had not deposed the Utrecht council, the Amsterdamers capitulated and turned the city – the last bastion of the 216-year-old United Republic – over to Kraijenhoff. That night the stadholder fled the country.

The reason why Adriaan de Lelie painted not the happenings in Amsterdam, but those in

Maarssen, may be sought in the circumstances of the presumable commission by the Nagel family. The young man behind Daendels, on the right, was Jan Nagel Jr., who was also being sent to Amsterdam by the general, but via another route. Had Kraijenhoff been detained underway, it may have been up to Jan Nagel to bring down the curtain on the United Republic. For 111 years, until the Nagels sold the painting to the Rijksmuseum, it served them as a conversation piece of the 'What

96

if...' variety. The mixture of homeliness and heroics in the painting corresponds well to the mood of the great but anti-climactic day itself.

The choice of Adriaan de Lelie for the commission was undoubtedly guided by considerations of revolutionary politics. De Lelie was one of the most prominent members of the Amsterdam artistic and philosophical society Felix Meritis, which was a gathering place for Patriot conspirators before the events of January 18th. He collaborated on several occasions with Egbert van Drielst, a decorative landscape painter who must have been considered a good Patriot as well: in 1799 he was paid 1,596 guilders for the restoration of paintings for the Museum of the Batavian Republic in The Hague, a job which would not have gone to anyone who had shown Orangist sympathies before 1795.

*NNBW*, vol. 1, col. 752. Niemeijer 1968, cat. nr. 2. Schama 1977, pp. 188-190.

The painting of sieges, for example, is related to a branch of art one could call military-artistic intelligence. The attics of the Musée des Invalides in Paris, the former officer training school of the French army, are still full of scale models of fortified cities and their natural surroundings. The military value of such material speaks for itself. The Dutch stadholders too were great believers in visual presentation. Maurits commissioned an illustrated manual for the use of the musket and pike which remained of value for two centuries, and his brother Frederik Hendrik liked all of his officers to be able to draw.

Membership in the military often inspired the understandable urge to be painted in one's uniform. The impulse seized groups as well as individuals, professional soldiers as well as members of the civic guard. The splendid ensign of the Orange company of the Hague civic guard (cat. nr. 37) was a burgher who spent his days practicing some trade or profession. Yet when he had his portrait painted, he chose to show himself not as a civilian but as the part-time soldier he also was. Apparently, soldiering takes precedence over other kinds of work in the self-image of the portrait sitter.

It would be a mistake, however, to place too much emphasis on the personal and psychological aspects of military portraiture. Convention and tradition too played a role of great importance. The family traditions of the nobility, for example, demanded that each successive male title-holder leave a portrait of himself in uniform for the gallery of ancestors in the family castle. This was the kind of tradition that exerted a mighty appeal on wealthy burghers as well. We know of an Amsterdam family of guardsmen, the Soops, in which the father and both of his sons had themselves painted in uniform (by Frans Hals and Rembrandt, no less).[1]

Conventions also guided the commissions for group portraits of military bodies. Those familiar images of guardsmen at banquets or other special occasions nearly all portray the same few bodies of the civic guard of Amsterdam, Haarlem and a few other cities of Holland, in the period 1550-1650. There are no such paintings of professional soldiers. The existing examples were made in the period when the civic guard was enjoying its greatest glory. The companies were composed of the leading citizens, and in the absence of representative government, they were the closest thing in many a city to a constituency of burghers. In Amsterdam, they thrived on the legendary events of the Alteration of 1578, when the newly formed companies of Calvinist guardsmen selected the members of the fresh town council. With the end of the Eighty Years War, the civic guard lost its unique importance, and the painting of group portraits came to a sudden end. A gallery of officers' portraits such as that of the twenty-four officers of the Orange-Friesland Regiment, all painted in the one year of 1731 (see nrs. 42-51), adds up to a group portrait of sorts. The overall effect of a wall of individual portraits, however, is purely decorative. No attempt is made to create the dramatic fiction of the seventeenth-century examples.

Engagements on land fought by the Dutch Republic tended to be battles of patience, which appealed to the popular imagination only if they looked like they were heading for a climax, and didn't last too long. Battles at sea were much more apt to raise temperatures to fever pitch. This was partly due to their dramatic structure: they were over in a few days if not hours, and nearly always were decisive. But there was another reason as well. The States army was a mixed group of professional soldiers from all over Europe, with few ties to the citizenry at large. Many of the officers were noblemen who, even if they were Netherlanders, spoke French in preference to Dutch. The sailors of the Dutch navy, on the other hand, came mostly from the backstreets of the cities of Holland, and the officers from their canals. On shore leave, they told stories about their experiences that brought the harbors of Ceylon and the Caribbean closer to home than the army camps of Drenthe and Zeeland. The admirals of the Dutch fleets, some of whose exploits were thrillingly indistinguishable from those of pirate kings, were deified as army commanders never were. In the words of a popular pamphlet, it was easier, in the Dutch Republic, to recruit a thousand sailors than a hundred soldiers.[2]

More or less the same ratio governed the market in paintings of sea versus land battles, of admirals versus generals. The leading specialists in military marine painting, artists like Willem van de Velde the older and younger (cat.nr. 41) and Ludolf Backhuysen, were always in demand. The van de Veldes were actually able to work alternately for the Dutch and English governments during the Anglo-Dutch Wars.

The registration of unusual day-to-day occurrences in art of a journalistic cast was not unknown in Holland, but it was generally confined to printmaking. There were a few kinds of natural prodigies which were always sure to draw a crowd of draughtsmen: stranded whales, broken dykes, plants of miraculous shape or size, fires, extreme frost; the kind of story which is still irresistible to the editors of television news programmes. The draughtsmen's sketches would be published quickly as prints or illustrations of broadsheets, but seldom did they make it into paint.

One kind of disaster which did become a small-scale painting specialty of its own was the explosion in a city. Two in particular: that of the powder magazine in Delft in 1654 (cat.nr. 39) and of a powder barge in Leiden in 1807 (cat.nr. 53). Of all the wonderful and terrible things that happened in Holland in those centuries, those two stuck out as particularly memorable, and paintable.

**53**

CAREL LODEWIJK
HANSEN (1765-1840),
figures partly by JACOB
SMIES (1764-1833)
*The Rapenburg, Leiden,
after the explosion, 1807.*
Signed *C.L. Hansen* and
inscribed *'t Raapenburg te
Leyden zo als het was 15
January 1807.* (The Ra-
penburg in Leiden as it
was on January 15, 1807).
Canvas, 94.5 × 125.5 cm.

The Netherlands Office
for Fine Arts, inv.nr. B
1288 (in the Academie-
gebouw, university of
Leiden). From the Pavilion

in Haarlem, as an exhibit
in the Rijksmuseum voor
Moderne Meesters (State
Museum for Living
Artists). Painted for King
Louis Napoleon, who
purchased it for the
National Museum in 1808.

On January 12, 1807, a
gunpowder barge being
tugged routinely through
the main canal of Leiden
by an inveterately careless
crew did what by rights it
should have done long
before: it blew up, taking a
good part of the neigh-
bourhood and many lives
with it. Three days later

King Louis Napoleon
visited the site. Hansen, in
a painting made for the
king, recorded what he
saw during the inspection,
probably including the
king himself and his en-
tourage in the scene. A
drawing by Hansen of the
site in the Leiden archives
is dated January 13.

The painting was pub-
lished in a print by F.
Diterich, with slight differences in the placing and
number of the function-
aries.

Hansen's attachment to
Louis Napoleon did not
prevent him from col-

laborating on the travel-
ling panorama of the
Battle of Waterloo.

Van Eijnden and van der
Willigen, vol.3, p.113,
note 1. Moes and van
Biema 1909, pp.132, 218.
Catalogues of the Laken-
hal, Leiden, 1949 (nr.122)
and Rijksmuseum,
Amsterdam, 1976, nr. A
3925.

**54**

MARTINUS SCHOUMAN
(1770-1848)
*The bombardment of Algiers
and the firing of the Algerian
fleet, August 26-27, 1816.*
Signed and dated
*M. Schouman f. 1823.*
Canvas, 95 × 159.5 cm.

Amsterdam, Rijks-
museum, inv.nr.A 1395.
From the model room of
the Ministry of Marine,
The Hague.

After the French occupa-
tion of their country, in
1813 the Dutch were once
again an independent
nation, though of a con-
siderably lower grade than
before the Napoleonic
period. Perhaps the
cruelest blow of all was

that Holland was no
longer a major maritime
power. Public morale was
therefore given a great
boost when in August
1816 the Dutch partici-
pated in a successful nine-
hour bombardment of
Algiers, under the English
admiral Exmouth, to en-
force the treaty abolishing
Christian slavery.

Schouman's painting of
the episode, dated seven
years after it took place, is
the same size as a canvas
by him of 1806, also from
the model room of the
Ministry of Marine, de-
picting a clash between the
Dutch and British fleets.
Significantly, the newer
work, which looks like it
was made to match the
earlier one, shows the

Dutch fighting not against
but under the British.

According to Schou-
man's contemporary bi-
ographer Immerzeel, a
painting of this subject by
the master was owned by
David van Poeliën, lord of
Nuland (1769-1830).
Poeliën was a fellow
Dordrecht townsman of
the artist, becoming one of
the first members of the
town council after the
founding of the Kingdom
in 1815 and acceding to
the burgomastership in
1824. A public benefactor
as well as a patron of the
arts, he contributed gen-
erously towards the aid of
soldiers maimed at Water-
loo. It would be
interesting to investigate
whether this painting was

a commission, inspired by
the patron's faith in the
English as allies and by his
humanitarian impulses.

Immerzeel, pp.78-79.
*NNBW*, vol.5, col.524.

**55**

JACOBUS SCHOEMAKER
DOYER (1792–1867)
*Lieutenant Jan van Speyk
pausing in thought before
detonating the powder keg in
the boat under his command
to keep it from falling to the
Belgians, February 5, 1831.*
Painted in 1834 for A. van
der Hoop after eyewitness
accounts by survivors.
Canvas, 89 × 75 cm.

Amsterdam, Rijks-
museum, inv.nr.C 221. On
loan from the city of
Amsterdam, to which it
was bequeathed with the
rest of the collection of
A. van der Hoop.

The highpoint of the Ten
Days Campaign was
painted at least three times
for Adriaan van der Hoop.
Schoemaker Doyer made a
companion painting of the
following moment, with
the hero kneeling to fire
the fateful shot, and
Schouman painted the
explosion itself, as seen
from a slight distance. All
three paintings are now in
the Rijksmuseum, on loan
from the city of Amster-
dam.

This canvas was ex-
hibited in 1834 under the
title 'Van Speyk having
made all the preparations
for igniting the powder,
stands introspectively as
two crewmen desert him.'
See the text.

Exhib. cat. *Het vaderlandsch
gevoel*, nr.65.

**56**

ARY SCHEFFER (1795–1858)
*Allons, enfants de la patrie.*
Dated 1825. Panel,
48 × 66.5 cm.

Dordrecht, Dordrechts Museum.

Ary Scheffer's father died when his son was only fourteen years old, in 1809. The father was court painter to the French King of Holland, Louis Napoleon, who offered to send the boy to France to complete his training as an artist. Before the family could take advantage of the offer, however, Louis Napoleon resigned. The widow took Ary to France on her own, starting him on a career that, after a very difficult start, was to become one of the most brilliant of the nineteenth century. Ary's brother Arnold became secretary to General Lafayette; both of them were conspicuous figures in the circle of the liberal duke of Orléans.

This sketch dates from the year after the restoration of the monarchy under the absolutist Charles x. A subject like *Allons, enfants de la patrie*, painted just as the privileges of the French aristocrats were being restored, was not calculated to inspire the trust of the powers that be. In fact, the Scheffer brothers were under surveillance by the secret police. They were to remain suspect until the coup of 1830 and the accession of the Roi Citoyen Louis Philippe, under whose reign they shined.

Kolb 1937.

On February 5, 1831 an incident took place which combined several of the above-mentioned ingredients for immortality in art, and which indeed did not fail to provide Dutch culture with a fetishistic new image. It occurred during the only fighting waged by the Kingdom of the Netherlands in the lowlands between the Battle of Waterloo against the French in 1815 and the invasion of the Germans in May 1940: the Ten Days Campaign against the Belgians, who had launched an uprising to gain independence from the Kingdom. The young, orphaned, lieutenant at sea Jan Carel Josephus van Speyk, unable to save the gunboat he was commanding, blew it sky-high rather than allow it to be taken. His patriotic sacrifice did not have to *become* a symbol – it was one, even in his mind, before it happened. Two months before his death, he wrote in a letter to his niece: 'In the meanwhile I must tell you (and I hope you will take me at my word) that the boat will be blown up, with powder, me and all, before becoming an infamous Brabander or being surrendered. I would rather be a Klaassen than a Deine.' The 'Klaassen' to whom the future hero was referring was the seventeenth-century vice-admiral Reinier Claasse, who in 1606 had blown up his ship rather than be taken by the Spaniards, while 'Deine' was a Dutch officer who in 1830 had deserted to Belgium.[3]

Van Speyk's prefabricated martyrdom was commemorated with phenomenal intensity. The details of his death were rehearsed, debated and glorified for years to come. In 1834, the collector Adriaan van der Hoop commissioned an authentic depiction of van Speyk's last moments from Jacobus Schoemaker Doyer (cat.nr.55). The artist based his depiction on the reports of a survivor, but was not able to keep his mind free of existing models, any more than was van Speyk himself.

1. Van Eeghen 1971.
2. Boxer 1965, p.80.
3. Exhib. cat. *Het vaderlandsch gevoel*, p.192, nr.65. De Leeuw 1985, p.17, refers to another prototype. In the play by M. Westerman, *Marco Bozzaris of de Grieken*, produced in Amsterdam in 1824, the hero, a Greek revolutionary leader, blows himself and his men up to avoid capture by the Turks.

# Scholarship, science and medicine

A fitting text for an essay on the relationship between painting and scholarship in Holland is provided by the historian Johannes Isacius Pontanus, professor of medicine and philosophy in Harderwijk, who introduced the painters of Amsterdam, in his *Historical description of the widely-famed merchant city Amsterdam* (1614), with the words: 'Painting is closely related to scholarship.' In his family, this was literally the case. His brother Pieter Isaacsz. was well-known as a painter and as one of the leading art dealers of Amsterdam. How correct he was in general, however, is a matter for debate, or even worse: a matter of opinion.

One of the problems with his thesis is illustrated by the difference the reader may have noticed between the form of his name and his brother's. In the style of the period when they were born, neither of them had a family name. They were given a Christian name, and after it came a patronymic. Because their father's first name was Isaac, the brothers both had the patronymic Isaacsz., standing for Isaacszoon, son of Isaac. When the younger brother, Jan, went to university and became a professional scholar, however, he followed the common practice of scholars in his time and Latinized his name, to Johannes Isacius. ('Pontanus' was an epithet alluding to Johannes's birth at sea.)

That is at the root of the problem: scholars were Latinists and painters were not. Scholars were citizens of the Republic of Letters. They communicated with each other throughout Europe in the universal language of learning, and shared a vast common store of knowledge. At the age of seven a future scholar would begin studying the classics while the future painter would be grinding pigments. If a painter expected to be able to conduct an intelligent conversation with a scholar on any subject but painting, he had a lot of catching up to do. One of the very few Dutch painters who regularly Latinized his name was Jan Lievens, of whom the learned Constantijn Huygens says that he could hold his own in discourse on 'the most miscellaneous subjects.' But Lievens was the younger brother of a Latin teacher, Titus Livius, and he himself an incurable boaster. The intellectual gap between painters and scholars is hard to imagine today, when many artists have the same kind of background in the liberal arts as specialist scholars, and may even hold the same academic rank. (Not in The Netherlands, though, where the creative arts are still kept out of the universities.)

The artists with whom some scholars did have regular contact were the draughtsmen and engravers who worked on book illustrations, which were

# The portrait gallery of Franeker University

The Frisian town of Franeker was the site of the second oldest institution of higher learning in the northern Netherlands, following Leiden by about ten years. After its founding in 1585 it quickly grew into a centre of considerable importance for the intellectual and ecclesiastical life of northern Europe. In the eighteenth century it suffered a decline, from which it may well have recovered were it not disbanded by Napoleonic decree in 1811.

Franeker was probably the first Dutch university to institute a formal gallery of professorial portraits in the Senate Chamber, where the professors met and academic ceremonies were conducted. The practice had been adopted, in varying forms, at several German universities in the sixteenth century, and in Leiden an informal collection had been initiated in 1597 by the librarian Paulus Merula. At Franeker the occasion for installing a gallery was provided, in all likelihood, by the restoration of the Senate Chamber, in a former monastery, in 1642. The plan was put into effect quite systematically. Portraits of a particular format and scale were commissioned, and an attempt was made to find likenesses of all the professors who had taught at the university since its establishment. This stage of the enterprise is undocumented, but in the light of what we know from later practice and records in other universities, the paintings were probably donated by the sitters or their families, while the university would pay for the frames and installation.

Because Franeker was still relatively young in 1642, the initiators of the gallery were able to gather a nearly complete set of portraits. In later years the example of Franeker was followed by other Dutch institutions of higher learning. Utrecht University established a formal gallery in its Senate Chamber upon its fiftieth anniversary in 1686, and was also able to achieve a high degree of completeness. When Leiden finally decided to regularize its policy, and to hang portraits of all professors in the Senate Chamber, it was already 1734-1735, and far too late in the day to assemble more than a random sampling of the first generations of professors.

We know something of the early arrangement of the portraits in Franeker from an account by the German traveler Zacharias von Uffenbach, who noted of the Senate Chamber in 1710 that it was 'the space where the Academic Senate, or the assembled professors, hold their meetings. It is rather large, and a nicer room than the one in Groningen. For one thing, you can plainly see – and it is a pleasure to do so – the portraits of fifty-two deceased professors ringing the room, the row being doubled here and there. Two are in the form of copper engravings only, behind glass. You find early professors and those recently deceased. Among them are some outstanding people, since, as is well known, this university has had the good fortune of having the best staff in nearly all faculties.'

As the portraits of generation after academic generation have accumulated in the surviving galleries in Utrecht, Leiden, Amsterdam and Groningen, the rows have long since turned into complete walls, so that Dutch Senate Chambers are plastered with professors. The individual portraits, many of them posthumous or copies after prints or family portraits, are much more diverse than a group like Accama's officer portraits, all by one painter in the same year, of men in identical uniforms (cat.nrs. 42-51). Moreover, university professors are probably more individualistic than army officers, and show it. Whether the modern visitor enjoys the effect as much as Uffenbach did depends strongly on the mood, temperament and circumstances of the observer.

In Franeker, the general policy was to hang portraits only of those who died or retired as full professors at the university. However, since Franeker did lose many of its best and brightest to the universities of Utrecht and Leiden, exceptions were allowed in favour of prominent figures who abandoned Friesland for the more sophisticated west of the country. Another exception was made for the portraits of three stadholders of Friesland, commissioned in 1721 from the young Bernardus Accama.

The professorial portrait gallery of Franeker was the first in the Netherlands to have a complete study devoted to it, by R.E.O. Ekkart. The above information is derived from that invaluable source. Ekkart traced all the portraits of Franeker professors he could locate, not just those from the Senate Chamber (which after a century in the city hall are now in the town museum, the Museum 't Coopmanshûs). He found portraits of four out of five of all those who had taught at the university.

Ekkart 1977.

**57**

ANONYMOUS

*Henricus Antonii Nerdenus, later called Henricus Antonides van der Linden (1546-1614).* Dated 1604. Copy of original by Jan Claesz. in private collection in Paris, where there is also a companion painting of the sitter's wife. Panel, 67.5 × 53 cm.

Franeker, Museum 't Coopmanshûs, inv.nr. Sch. 15. From the Senate Chamber of Franeker University.

Professor of theology at Franeker from the founding of the university in 1585 until his death. A pedagogical theologian, who was more concerned with the training of ministers and academic life than with the dogmatic disputes of his time.

*NNBW*, vol. 8, col. 1058. Ekkart 1977, nr. 6.

**58**

ANONYMOUS

*Joannes Drusius (1550-1616).* Dated 1606. Canvas, 66.5 × 55 cm.

Franeker, Museum 't Coopmanshûs, inv. nr. Sch. 16. From the Senate Chamber of Franeker University.

Drusius's father was a Flemish Protestant, his mother a Catholic. When the family was torn apart in the religious troubles, he chose his father's creed, and fled to England, where he studied Oriental languages so brilliantly that he was offered professorships by Oxford and Cambridge at the age of 22. In 1577 he accepted a chair in Oriental languages in the new university of Leiden, but was paid so poorly that he left for Franeker in 1585, where he earned five hundred guilders a year. There he remained for the rest of a highly productive life, despite the antagonism of his dogmatic Calvinist colleagues, who suspected him of being a Remonstrant. The unrelenting antagonism of Lubbertus is said to have led to his sudden death. His collected works were published in ten volumes in 1622-1636.

*NNBW*, vol. 1, cols. 753-757. Ekkart 1977, nr. 17.

**59**

ANONYMOUS

*Sibrandus Lubbertus (1556-1625).* Dated 1616. Panel, 67 × 54 cm.

Franeker, Museum 't Coopmanshûs, inv. nr. Sch. 14. From the Senate Chamber of Franeker University.

Professor of theology at Franeker from 1585 until his death forty years later, Lubbertus was a hard worker, who was said to begin writing at three o'clock in the morning. He had no academic experience when he came to Franeker from a post as itinerant minister for the States of Friesland. At the university he appointed himself watch-dog of good morals and right thinking, driving his colleagues Maccovius and Drusius to despair. Lubbertus was even stricter than the leader of his own Counter-Remonstrant party, Franciscus Gomarus, whom he accused of unorthodox tendencies. At the Synod of Dordt, where the States General allowed the Counter-Remonstrants to condemn the Remonstrants, Lubbertus was much in evidence.

*NNBW*, vol. 2, cols. 843-849. Ekkart 1977, nr. 1.

**60**

ANONYMOUS

*Meinardus Schotanus (1593-1644).* Painted after a lost portrait of 1641 by J. van Zuylen or a print after that portrait. Canvas, 66.5 × 54 cm.

Franeker, Museum 't Coopmanshûs, inv. nr. Sch. 3. From the Senate Chamber of Franeker University.

The sitter was a theologian from a family of jurists. His father Henricus taught law, as did his brother Bernardus. Meinardus was an orthodox Calvinist who was much sought after as a preacher. He filled a chair in theology in Franeker from 1620 to 1632, when he accepted a chancel in Leeuwarden. He returned to the academic life in 1636 in Franeker, moving on quickly, in 1637, to Utrecht. There he became the ally of Gisbertus Voetius in a 'theological triangle' whose third leg was Carolus de Maets.

*NNBW*, vol. 9, cols. 1000-1001. Ekkart 1977, nr. 74.

**61**

ANONYMOUS
*Johannes Coccejus (1603-1669)*. Copy after original of about 1666 in Amsterdam University by Anthonie Palamedesz. Canvas, 86 × 67.5 cm.

Franeker, Museum 't Coopmanshus, inv.nr. Sch.33. From the Senate Chamber of Franeker University.

Coccejus had a reputation as a brilliant student of Hebrew, Arabic, Turkish and, especially, Talmudic Aramaic when he came to Franeker to study in 1626. In 1630 he took a chair in his native Bremen, but returned to Franeker as professor of Oriental lan-guages in 1636. In 1650 he moved on to the university of Leiden. His philological approach to Scripture led him into a vicious polemic with his Utrecht colleague Gisbertus Voetius, who read the New Testament as a succession of dogmas. When they crossed swords in 1659 over the issue of the Sabbath, feelings ran so high that the States General had to forbid preaching on the subject to prevent a new schism in the church.

*NNBW*, vol. 1, cols. 616-618. Ekkart 1977, nr. 103.

**62**

BERNARDUS ACCAMA
(1697-1756)
*Zacharias Huber (1669-1732)*. Dated 1728. Canvas, 84 × 66 cm.

Franeker, Museum 't Coopmanshûs, inv.nr. Sch. 130. From the Senate Chamber of Franeker University.

Zacharias Huber was the son of the leading Franeker professor of law, Ulricus Huber, whom he succeeded in 1695 after four years of law practice in Leeuwarden. Zacharias filled the chair for twenty-two years, before leaving to become an advocate at the court of Friesland in 1716. In his teaching he stressed the importance of the classics for the practice of law, while in his later writings he devoted more attention to contemporary legal developments.

*NNBW*, vol. 1, cols. 1168-1169. Ekkart 1977, nr.256.

TIBERIUS HEMSTERHUIS.

**63**

JAN PALTHE (1717-1769)
*Tiberius Hemsterhuis (1685-1766).* Dated 1757. Canvas, 77 × 61 cm.

Leiden, Rijksuniversiteit. In the Senate Chamber of Leiden University since 1774 or earlier.

The son of a distinguished Frisian doctor, Hemsterhuis was recognized as a child prodigy. At the age of thirteen he entered the university of Groningen, where he studied mathematics, Greek, Hebrew and theology. At the age of nineteen, in 1704, he became professor of philosophy and mathematics at the school of higher learning (not yet a university) in Amsterdam, but a serious conflict with the board, probably of a political nature, led to his quick departure. In 1717 he was appointed professor of Greek at Franeker. He also taught Dutch history (one of his students was the son of the Frisian stadholder), from 1738 on as professor. In 1740 he accepted a chair in Leiden, where he served several terms as rector, and addressed Stadholder Willem IV in the name of the university senate. His scholarly reputation was based mainly on his contributions to the study of ancient Greek, which he treated separately from the Oriental languages.

*NNBW*, vol. I, cols. 1068-1072. Ekkart 1977, nr. 279.

**64**

HIERONYMUS VAN DER MIJ (1687-1761)
*Albert Schultens (1686-1750).* Dated 1736. Canvas, 76.5 × 61 cm.

Leiden, Rijksuniversiteit. Commissioned by the sitter for the Senate Chamber of Leiden University.

When Schultens became professor of Hebrew and Antiquities (Archaeology) at Franeker University in 1713, he began to put into practice a system of study he had conceived when he was not yet twenty years old: comparative Semitic philology as the basis for Bible study. If Coccejus read the Bible as a product of human literary effort, Schultens went a step further, to see the very language of the Bible, old Hebrew, as a minor branch in a larger family of languages which was dominated by Arabic. In 1729 he was called to Leiden as regent of the prestigious States College, and in 1732 was appointed professor of Oriental languages. His new approach to ancient Semitic texts was not understood and appreciated by all, but the polemics in which he participated were far more scholarly and less vindictive than those in which his seventeenth-century predecessors found themselves engaged.

*NNBW*, vol. 5, cols. 707-711. Ekkart 1977, nr. 269.

**65**

TIBOUT REGTERS (1710-1768)
*Nicolaas Ypey (1714-1785).*
Dated 1763. Canvas,
85 × 70 cm.

Franeker, Museum 't
Coôpmanshus, inv. nr.
Sch. 108. From the
Ypey family collection.
Presented in 1972 by Mrs.
W. E. Ypey to the Fries
Museum, Leeuwarden. On
loan to the Franeker
museum.

Ypey studied in Franeker
and Leiden before going to
Paris, where he followed
courses in military fortification. He succeeded one
of his teachers in Franeker
as lecturer and then professor, teaching and publishing

on fortification, mathematics, astronomy, economics
and political science.

*NNBW*, vol. 5, cols. 1161-
1162. Ekkart 1977, nr. 324.

**66**

TIBOUT REGTERS (1710-1768)
*Bavius Voorda (1729-1799).*
Painted about 1765. Can-
vas, 76 × 60 cm.

Leiden, Rijksuniversiteit.
Presented in 1799 by the
sitter's brothers.

Voorda was born in Frane-
ker, the son of a jurist and
law professor who had studied under Zacharias
Huber (nr. 62). After
studying law in Utrecht
and Leiden, he began his
career with a practice in
Leeuwarden, which he
abandoned for a thousand-
guilder-a-year chair at Franeker University in 1755.
In 1765 he moved on to
Leiden, where, as in Frane-

ker, he filled the high post
of rector.

In 1788 Voorda ran
afoul of the authorities for
his Patriotic sentiments,
and was relieved of his
professorship. With the
establishment of the Batavian Republic in 1795 he
returned in glory, choos-
ing the university over a
judgeship in the high court
of Holland which he was
also offered. He enjoyed
the satisfaction of seeing
his charge of treason
against the deposed stad-
holder adopted by the
national assembly.

*NNBW*, vol. 3, cols. 1335-
1338. Ekkart 1977, nr. 383.

**67**

NICOLAES MAES (1634–1693)
*Gisbertus Voetius (1589–1676)*. Canvas, 44 × 34 cm. Model for the painting in the Senate Chamber of Utrecht University.

Utrecht, Universiteitsmuseum (on loan to Rijksmuseum Het Catharijneconvent, Utrecht). Acquired about 1964.

For half a century, Gijsbert Voet, with the zeal of an ayatollah, protected the principles of 'the true Reformed Christian religion' against the influence of Catholicism, Anabaptism, Judaism, Remonstrantism, Cartesianism, Jansenism, Labadism and backsliding leaders of his own creed of Calvinism. He was an ecclesiastical politician, a minister, a dogmatician, and an academic, in that order. When the Utrecht school of higher education became a university in 1636, he was appointed professor of theology, a chair which he accepted with an inaugural address on 'joining piety with science.' Under his unwavering leadership, the Utrecht faculty of theology took over the lead from Leiden as the heartland of intransigent Calvinism.

However over-pronounced his stance, Voetius was not a caricature of a man. He was exception-

ally intelligent and clear-thinking, had a taste for music and a weakness for Anna Maria van Schuurman. Some traces of his impact on the outside world can be found in the entries above, on Schotanus and Coccejus, and below, on Anna Maria van Schuurman.

His portrait is by one of the best Dutch painters ever to paint an academic portrait, the Rembrandt pupil Nicolaes Maes.

Duker 1897–1915.

## 68

MICHIEL VAN MIEREVELT
(1567-1641)
*Anna Maria van Schuurman
(1607-1678).* Panel, 63 × 52
cm.

Franeker, Museum
't Coopmanshûs, inv.nr.
Sch. 52

Anna Maria van Schuur-
man was the exception
that proves the rule that
women played no role in
the Dutch world of learn-
ing. Her linguistic gifts
(she commanded a
scholar's knowledge of the
modern languages as well
as Latin, Greek, Hebrew,
Syriac and Arabic) and
her correspondence with
scholars all over Europe
earned her fame and
respect. She was also a
painter, engraver and
embroiderer of exceptional
talent; in 1641 she was
admitted to the Utrecht
guild of St. Luke.

From 1623 to 1632
Anna Maria lived in
Franeker, where she made
the acquaintance of René
Descartes, and came un-
der the influence of his
humanistic philosophy.
Eventually, however, she
moved back to Utrecht
and to the camp of her old
and constant protector
Gisbertus Voetius, the fire-
breathing Calvinist, who
arranged for her to be able
to follow lectures at the
university when it opened
in 1636. An academic
position was however out
of the question, and Anna

Maria had to do without
the durability of an official
appointment.

When her mother died
in 1647, she became
responsible for two aged
aunts, a task which took
her away from the uni-
versity. She began prac-
ticing a more personal
form of worship than
ecclesiastical Calvinism,
and in the 1660s became a
devoted follower of the
Swiss pietist Jean de La-

badie. When he moved to
Holland in 1666, she
joined her lot with his,
even taking the daring step
of living in his house in
Amsterdam. The group
around Labadie was chased
from pillar to post in
Holland, Germany and
Denmark. After the death
of the founder, Anna
Maria became co-leader of
the independent sect of
Labadists, in the Frisian
town of Wiewerd.

G.D.J. Schotel, *Anna
Maria van Schuurman*, 's-
Hertogenbosch 1853.
*NNBW*, vol. 1, cols. 1465-
1466; information from
the museum.

**69**

WERNER VAN DEN
VALCKERT (?; ca. 1560/65 –
after 1627)
*The anatomy lecture of Dr.*
*Sebastiaan Egbertsz. de Vrij*
*(1563-1621).* Painted in
1619. Canvas, 135 × 186
cm.

Amsterdam, Amsterdams
Historisch Museum, cat.
nr. 210, inv. nr. A 7352.
Presented to the city in
1864 by an ad hoc Com-
mittee of Art Lovers,
Artists and Physicians,
after the city, in 1862, had
permitted it to be sold,
with fourteen other
paintings belonging to the

surgeons' guild, to a private individual.

This is the second painting
of an anatomical demon-
stration by the prelector
of the Amsterdam sur-
geons' guild. The first one
dates from 1603, and
portrays the same Sebas-
tiaan Egbertsz., who held
the post from 1595 until
his death. The repetition
established a tradition
from which Rembrandt
benefitted in 1632, when
he painted the fourth
painting of this kind for
the guild, the famous
*Anatomy lecture of Dr.*
*Nicolaas Tulp.*

Both paintings of anat-
omy lectures by Sebastiaan
Egbertsz. followed upon
important events in his
political career. (Even
before he became guild
prelector, he had served a
term as alderman, and in
1606 and 1608 he was
burgomaster.) In 1602, he
entered the town council,
and in 1618 he was ejected
from it. The ejection was
the result of Sebastiaan's
siding with the Remon-
strants, an attitude one
would not expect from the
son of one of the most
militant Calvinists in pre-
Reformation Amsterdam,
who escaped being

executed by the Spaniards
only by dying in prison
the night before.

An event in the history
of the guild of which he
was such an important
member no doubt also
gave an impulse to the
painting of a second
anatomy lecture by Se-
bastiaan Egbertsz. In April
1619 he opened a new
anatomical theatre, above
the weighing hall in the
former St. Anthony's
Gate, premises which the
surgeons shared with the
painters of the guild of St.
Luke.

From 1746 until 1983,
the painting was thought

to be the earliest work by Thomas de Keyser, son of the town architect and sculptor Hendrick de Keyser. In a recent article, however, Pieter van Thiel has removed it, with convincing arguments, from de Keyser's work and assigned it tentatively to Werner van den Valckert. The attribution certainly makes good sense from the point of view of patronage politics. Van den Valckert, who lived on the square outside St. Anthony's Gate and was probably a guild officer, was a painter to the Catholics and Remonstrants of Amsterdam, like Sebastiaan Egbertsz.

The painting is a brilliant performance, introducing into Dutch group portraiture a new kind of dynamism and unity, enriched with a sense of humour.

Elias, vol. I, pp. 258-260. Van Thiel 1983.

reluctantly accepted as instruments for the transmission of knowledge. Engravers were expected to be literate, and to have at least a rudimentary understanding of the works for which they provided title plates or figures. This narrow basis for professional collaboration was cultivated energetically by a few Dutch scholars, though most had no desire to have their books illustrated or to have any other kind of contact with art.

The prejudice had many roots, the deepest of which was intellectual mistrust. In the section on religion we noted that the Calvinists valued texts above images as vehicles for imparting knowledge. This standpoint also prevailed at the universities, most of which were bulwarks of Calvinism. The issue was not only theological, however, but also cognitive. Texts are built up from discrete elements which can be examined minutely for technical correctness and truth to fact. Pictures can seldom be analyzed this way. Even those which appear to be models of straightforward description break down, under close observation, into mere spots and strokes of colour. Whatever lifelikeness they possess is plainly an illusion. To the lovers of strict interpretation that Dutch scholars tended to be, this in itself was enough to discredit painting as a partner for learning. The art of drawing, in which a line on paper may correspond to the measurable contour of an object in nature, was regarded with somewhat less suspicion. These are manifestations of what one could call 'cultural class.' (Before dismissing them as the biases of a quaint age long past, reader, you may want to ask yourself why you believe that reading a book is a more worthwhile activity than watching television.)

Social class played less of a role. Painters, like scholars, tended to come from the upper middle ranks of society; families like those of the brothers Jan and Pieter Isaacsz. and Jan and Titus Lievens were not all that exceptional. The brother of Lievens's own master Joris van Schooten was a professor at the University of Leiden – the first one to teach in the vernacular rather than Latin.

Professional stigma, on the other hand, *was* an important divider. When an academic got drunk or was involved in a scandal, he disgraced his calling. A painter who misbehaved was only living up to expectations. Whether or not the stereotype was earned I cannot say. But it certainly existed. The pious Mennonite father of Govert Flinck prayed to God that his son would not become a painter, 'most of them being bohemians and wantons.' (One of the rare university professors who was also a serious artist, the botanist, classicist and etcher Joannes Brosterhuysen, was constantly in trouble for excessive drinking and for living in sin with his housekeeper.) Even young men to whom this was only an added attraction may have been put off by another aspect of the painter's image: that he wore a smock and always had dirty hands, like a common worker.

**70-73**
Attributed to WERNER
VAN DEN VALCKERT
A series of four paintings:
*The physician as God*; *The
physician as an angel*; *The
physician as a man*; and *The
physician as the devil*.
Panels, each ca. 95 × 96.5
cm.

Leiden, Museum Boer-
haave, inv. nrs. 811-814.
Together with nrs. 71-73,
purchased for the museum
at sale London (Christie's),
July 2, 1976, with support
from the Vereniging
Rembrandt. The panels
come from the collection
of Count Otto Thot,

Gaunø Castle, near Noar-
sted, Denmark, where
they have been since 1785.

The physician is seen
through the eyes of the
patient in these four successive scenes: to the
patient who has given
himself up, the healer who

saves his life is God himself. As long as he is ill, the
patient will see his attending physician as an angel,
and the convalescent will
see him like a man. When
the patient has recovered,
however, and the doctor
comes to present his bill,
he becomes the devil
incarnate.

The paintings are based on a suite of four engravings brought out by Hendrick Goltzius in 1587, but there are too many differences between the paintings and the prints for the former to be considered mere painted copies. Moreover, the difference in medium is very important. Four prints of an amusing and human subject like this, executed with such a fascinating wealth of detail, could be sold to anyone, but a series of large, precious paintings must have been made for a wealthy patron, most likely an individual physician or a guild.

The depiction of the instruments alone, which are shown with a great measure of accuracy, must have demanded considerable cooperation between the artist and a medical man. Moreover, the backgrounds of the paintings show three case histories in paint: a fever patient, one with a broken leg, and a third being treated by trepanation, boring a hole in the skull.

The texts in the books on the final painting reinforce our feeling that the

series was a kind of advertisement for the medical profession.

The attribution to Werner van den Valckert has not been accepted by the most recent author on the master, Pieter van Thiel. No new name has as yet been proposed. The Danish provenance of the painting reminds us of the lively export to Scandinavia of Dutch paintings throughout the seventeenth century. There were even ambitious series of paintings commissioned by Scandinavian patrons from Dutch painters – including one for the King of Denmark on which Werner van den Valckert worked.

Museum information, with kind thanks to Peter de Clercq.

**74**

Attributed to ARIE DE VOIS (ca. 1632-1680)
*The scholar Adriaan van Beverland with a prostitute.*
Inscribed *Beverlandus de Prostibulis Veterum* (Beverland, On the brothel in antiquity). Probably painted in 1678 (see below). Panel, 35 × 27.5 cm.

Amsterdam, Rijksmuseum, inv.nr. A 3237. Acquired in 1935 with the bequest of F.G. Waller (1867-1934), a wealthy art historian, collector and near-recluse who left most of his property to the nation. The F.G. Waller Fund is still the main source of income for acquisitions by the Rijksmuseum printroom.

If the subject is provocative, it was intended to be. Adriaan van Beverland (ca. 1652-ca. 1712), the grandson of a minister and the son and stepson of high military officers, was a gadfly. He was a serious collector of erotica, but unlike most of that tribe, who enjoy their holdings in private, he insisted on publicizing his, and doing so as mockingly as possible. He mounted obscene engravings on sheets of paper and provided them with texts from ancient authors, announcing his intention of publishing the collection as a contribution to humanistic studies, under

the title *On the brothel in antiquity*. This plan was interrupted, however, by the reaction to another of his books, *Peccatum originale*, subtitled 'The so-called original sin.' His thesis, based on Scripture, that the crime of Adam and Eve was coitus, was bad enough, but the consequences he attached to it

– that *all* sexual intercourse was sinful – led to his incarceration in the Leiden university jail, in 1679. When he was released he moved to Utrecht, where he showed the material for *On the brothel in antiquity*, including a title print with the same composition as this painting. The print bears the inscriptions

*Hadrianus Beverlandus Aet. XXVI*, yielding the date 1678, and *J. de Vois pinxit* (after a model painted by J. de Vois), which is the basis of the attribution to Arie de Vois, the only known painter with that family name. Neither the style nor the little we know about the artist's life counters the plausibility of

A form of painting which university professors did consider appropriate for the adornment of their buildings were portraits of themselves. This characteristic feature of the Dutch academic environment, which has continued as a living institution to our day, is represented in the exhibition with seven portraits from one of the most handsome of these series, that of the former University of Franeker in Friesland, and three from Leiden (cat.nrs. 57-66).

The relative lack of interest displayed by scholars in painters was mutual. In the exhibition is included the only known Dutch seventeenth-century painting of an academic ceremony (cat.nr. 76). When Dutch artists of that period showed scholars at their work, they usually fell back on old stereotypes of the philosopher or alchemist. Men of letters who were not professional scholars would sometimes have themselves painted with attributes of learning, but scholars did so rarely.

The very institutions of their profession kept artists at a distance from scholars. The older guilds of the Republic usually lumped the painters together with the housepainters, glaziers and other less creative craftsmen. (Engravers, on the other hand, often belonged to the booksellers' guild, which of course *was* an important institution for universities and their professors.) There was a perennial striving on the part of artists to rise above their colleagues 'of the big brush,' to found academies and confraternities where they could be among themselves and talk about the higher things in art and life. But this movement was kept in check by other forces. When they left the guilds, painters had to establish new ties with the civic authorities for the protection of their rights, and this was not a simple matter. Moreover, most Dutch painters really did have more in common with their colleagues in the broad-based guild than with the serious students of culture in the academies.

It was not until the Age of Reason and beyond that societies were established, outside the strictly professional sphere, for painters *and* scholars. The most successful example is the eighteenth-century Teylers Foundation, whose survival to our day, complete with its cabinet of art and science, must be considered a miracle. More typical was the Royal Institute, founded in 1808, and still the leading learned society of the Netherlands, whose Fourth Division, for artists, was disbanded in 1851.

de Vois's authorship of the painting. The nineteenth-century artist's biographer Christiaan Kramm went so far as to endorse the attribution with the remark 'Birds of a feather flock together.'

Kramm, vol. 6, pp. 1784-1785. Meijer 1971.

Ties between painters and the world of medicine were not all that much more fruitful. The medical faculties were among the first departments of the universities to make their peace with draughtsmen and engravers for the illustration of handbooks, but seldom turned to painters for any purpose but portraiture. The surgeons of Amsterdam, who were less academic than the university anatomists of Leiden, struck a fascinating compromise. They initiated the practice of portraying themselves not at a meal or as a row of

**75**

EGBERT VAN
HEEMSKERCK (ca. 1634–
1704)
*The surgeon-barber Jacob
Fransz. Hercules and his
family*. Signed and dated
*HKerck 1669*. Canvas,
70 × 59 cm.

Amsterdam, Amsterdams
Historisch Museum,

cat. nr. 170, inv. nr. 2121.
Purchased in 1948 from
the Governors of the
Oranje Appel (Orange)
Orphanage, Amsterdam,
who probably received it
from the heirs of Willem
van Aelst Willemsz. after
his death in 1774. The
Oranje Appel was the
meeting place of the
Amsterdam Collegiants, a

dissident sect founded in
1618, to which Jacob
Fransz. Hercules and his
family also belonged.

The museum preserves a
detailed note by Willem
van Aelst Willemsz. which
was formerly attached to
the back of the painting,
and which identifies the
figures: 'Portrayal of the

family of my mother
Geertruid Hercules. The
person letting blood is
Jacob Fransz. Hercules my
grandfather, †1707. The
person being bled is his
brother Thomas Hercules,
†1695. Holding the basin
is Jacob Fransz.'s son
Thomas Jacobsz. Hercules,
my mother's brother...'
and so forth. The man

122

reading the newspaper is identified as 'the notorious Jan Knol,' a reformed criminal who became a pietist preacher, which got him into as much trouble as his former line of trade.

Hercules Fransz. was a music-lover and art collector, whose inventory included works by Rembrandt.

In the catalogue of the Amsterdam Historical Museum, the painting is said to be the only known depiction of the shop of a middle-class professional. The artist must have been a friend of the family. His usual work shows peasants and soldiers in taverns, though he also painted scenes of sorcery and temptations of St. Anthony. A certain thematic connection with this work can be sensed in his depictions of Quaker meetings in England, and one of a prisoner repenting. Not too long after painting the Hercules family, the artist left for England, where he became a favourite of the Earl of Rochester, who shared van Heemskerck's interests in spiritualism and dissipation. As George Vertue put it in his *Notebooks*, 'He was a man of Humour, and for that Valu'd by the late Earl of Rochester.'

Wurzbach, vol. I, pp.658–659. White 1982, under Heemskerck.

heads, but as listeners at a lecture of the guild anatomist (cat.nr.69). This tradition offered painters a chance to demonstrate the value of their art as an aid to learning. The most ambitious attempt in this direction was Rembrandt's *Anatomy lecture of Dr. Nicolaes Tulp* (1632), which shows the surgeon dissecting an arm. The choice of this limb has been interpreted by William Heckscher, in his book on the painting, as a demonstration that manual dexterity lies behind the miracles performed by the surgeon as well as the painter. If there was one group of surgeons in the country which would have been susceptible to this heretical argument, it would have been the Amsterdam surgeons' guild. The guild anatomy theatre was located in the same former city gate where the painters' guild had its headquarters, and many members had an interest in the arts.

The medical profession was divided between university-trained doctors and unlettered popular practitioners who were often barbers as well as surgeons (cat.nr.75). The latter were more important for painters, if only because serious paintings of the medical profession are few in number compared to the many genre paintings making fun of barber-surgeons, quacks and their patients. Even the academically trained doctors seldom get a chance to show off their expensive knowledge. When a physician appears in a painting of a Dutch household, he has nearly always been called in to diagnose a feverish young woman, which he does by holding up a flask of her urine to the light. In ways that are sometimes witty and sometimes coarse, the painter manages to suggest to the viewer that the young lady is lovesick or pregnant. In this function, the doctor was called by the homespun name 'The piss-inspector.'

Bodily functions and the suspicion of illicit sex are also the subjects of a pair of medical paintings by the foremost eighteenth-century Dutch painter, Cornelis Troost (cat.nrs.78–79). On a visit to a lady patient of middle age, a doctor is demonstrating to the complete household the proper motion for administering an enema with a syringe. In the companion painting, the doctor attends a woman newly delivered of a baby which her soldier husband holds up beside his own reflection to assure himself of the paternal resemblance. Troost was an actor on the Amsterdam stage and a painter of decors, and many of his works reveal his involvement with the theatre.

The theatre was in fact a middle ground between the worlds of painting and of learning. Although playwrights and poets who wrote in Dutch rather than Latin were not necessarily considered scholars themselves, many of them were taken seriously by the world of learning. And they in turn collaborated in various ways with painters. The best example is Jan Vos, who was the protégé of one of the founding professors of the university of Amsterdam, Caspar Barlaeus, and who, as director of the town theatre, was always working with painters. That did not speak for itself.

**76**

HENDRICK VAN DER
BURGH (active mid-seven-
teenth century)
*An academic ceremony in
Leiden.* Signed *JVB.* Can-
vas, 71.5 × 59 cm.

Amsterdam, Rijksmu-
seum, inv.nr. A 2720. Purchased in 1915 from J.H.
Langeveldt, Voorhout.

This may be the only
surviving seventeenth-cen-

tury painting of an
academic ceremony in the
Netherlands. The building
which the procession is
leaving is still the site of
academic ceremonies at
Leiden University.

**77**

JURRIAAN POOL (1666–1745)
*Two officers of the Amsterdam surgeons' guild, probably A. Boekelman and Jan Six.* Signed and dated *JPool f 1699.* Canvas, 73 × 114 cm.

Amsterdam, Amsterdams Historisch Museum, cat.nr. 346, inv.nr. A 3031 (on loan to Museum Boerhaave, Leiden). Presented to the city in 1864 under the same circumstances as cat. nr. 69).

Looking at this painting next to Werner van der Valckert's group portrait with skeleton of eighty years earlier, we feel ourselves present at the transition from the age of the generalist to that of the specialist. The earlier anatomical portraits still seem to exemplify a religious message such as the one put into words by Joost van den Vondel, in his poem on Cornelis Plemp's translation into Dutch of an anatomical textbook by Cabrious:

'Know thyself' were
    words engraved
Above a Delphic archi-
    trave
As enlightenment divine
From the mistress of that
    shrine.
Today the same is taught
    to us
By doctors like wise
    Cabrious...
He who seeks to com-
    prehend
From beginning until end
What our human skins
    encase,
What keeps all our parts in
    place,
How the wisdom of the
    Lord obtains
Throughout our nerves,
    throughout our veins,
How artists all are put to
    shame
By the artful human
    frame –
Should he help one man
    succeed
To know himself and then
    proceed
To knowledge of God's
    nature too,
Then Plemp will feel he's
    had his due.

Pool's painting, on the contrary, looks more like a consultation between a heart specialist and a medical technician on a matter that touches both their fields.

The painter was not a stranger to the world of the sitters. He was the son-in-law, since 1695, of one of the foremost physicians in the city, Frederick Ruysch. Mevrouw Pool was Rachel Ruysch, herself an outstanding flower painter.

Schwartz 1965, p. 144.

**78**

CORNELIS TROOST (1697–
1750)
*The doctor's visit.* Canvas,
81.5 × 104 cm.

and

**79**

*The newborn child being
admired by its father.*
Canvas, 83.5 × 103 cm.

The Netherlands Office
for Fine Arts, inv.nrs. NK
1435 and 1434, respec-
tively (on loan to Stedelijk
Museum Het Catharina-
gasthuis, Gouda). From

the Goudstikker gallery
(see nr. 21).

The two paintings have
always been kept together,
and were probably made
as companion pieces,
although it is not easy to
put one's finger on their
thematic link. Perhaps
they illustrate two scenes
from an as yet unidentified
play. See the text.

80

PAUL CONSTANTIJN LA
FARGUE (1729-1782)
*The meeting hall of Kunst
Wordt door Arbeid Ver-
kregen.* Signed and dated
*P.C. la Fargue pinx 1774.*
Canvas, 59 × 73.5 cm.

Leiden, Stedelijk Museum
De Lakenhal, inv.nr.900a
(purchased in 1952 from
R. Kneppelhout van
Sterkenburg; another
painting of the same room
by the same artist, dated
1780, was donated in the
year of purchase by Mr.
Kneppelhout to the

Rijksmuseum [inv.nr.A
3834], and has been on
loan to the Lakenhal since
1959).

Kunst Wordt door Arbeid
Verkregen – Art is At-
tained through Labour –
was the name of a minor
society of the arts which
met in Leiden from 1766
to 1800. Its two main
distinctions are both visible
in this painting: the de-
lightful premises where the
society gathered until
1780, and, against the back
wall, the cabinet of min-
iature paintings of Dutch

poets, the Panpoeticon
Batavum.

The meeting hall was a
room in the house of the
Leiden bookseller Cornelis
van Hoogeveen (1740-
1792), whose many
memberships in literary
societies are said to have
brought on his ruin.

The Panpoeticon con-
tained three hundred and
fifty portraits, of which
some two hundred were
copied from prints by the
founder of the collection,
Arnoud van Halen (1673-
1732). Kunst Wordt door
Arbeid Verkregen, after

attempting in vain to
interest King Louis
Napoleon in buying the
cabinet and its contents,
sold them at auction. In
later years they were dispersed. Today the Rijks-
museum owns 78 of the
miniatures; the cabinet has
disappeared.

Paul Constantijn la
Fargue was a member of
Kunst Wordt door Arbeid
Verkregen. He began
work on this painting in
1771 and finished it three
years later. In 1780, when
van Hoogeveen had to ask
the society to leave his

Before the middle of the seventeenth century, theoretical writings about art invariably ranked poetry above painting. The art of painting did not even have a muse for itself among the nine who surrounded Apollo on Parnassus. They brought 'to humanity the purifying power of music, the inspiration of poetry, and divine wisdom.'[1] Next to that, the sensual pleasure provided by painting does not make a very elevated impression. In poetry the divine and human spirit is made manifest in the word, while painting turns spirit into matter. In the rhetoric of art theory, painting was the tenth, non-canonical muse, who was accommodated on Parnassus thanks to the obligingness of the real arts. Re-translated into terms of everyday life, this meant that a poet who associated with painters was slumming. Jan Vos did not think it was beneath his dignity, but many more did.

Support of a much heavier calibre came from abroad, from France. There, the claims of painting were accorded full recognition with the inclusion of painters in the new Academy, founded in 1648. The first full-scale treatise on painting written in Holland after that year, by the painter Samuel van Hoogstraten, came out in 1678 under the title *Introduction to the Academy of Painting* (Inleyding tot de Hooge Schoole der Schilderkonst), and it was divided into nine books, each corresponding to a muse. Painting had become the mistress of Parnassus.

The debate concerning the place of painting among the arts and sciences touched some essential aspects of the artistic life. To the eye of the twentieth-century viewer, the issue seems to have been resolved by history in the favour of painting. The work of seventeenth-century Dutch painters is still prized by all the world and traded for fortunes of money, while the poets of the period have been pushed off to a stuffy corner of specialist scholarship. But that is not an answer to all the questions in the debate, some of which have flared up again in our own time in a discussion between Dutch and American scholars. They disagree on the balance between the intellectual and sensual components of Dutch painting. To their clash of opinions we will return in the final section of the exhibition.

house, la Fargue painted his second view of the room, seen from the other side.

For the painting, see cat. De Lakenhal 1983; for the Panpoeticon Batavum, cat. Rijksmuseum 1976, pp.723-736; for van Hoogeveen, *NNBW*, vol.5, col.242; for Kunst Wordt door Arbeid Verkregen, Pelinck 1956.

1. *The Oxford classical dictionary*, 1973, p.704.

**81**

HENDRICK VROOM
(1566-1640)
*View of Delft,* 1634.
Canvas, 71 × 162 cm.

Delft, Museum Het Prinsenhof, inv.nr.s 131. Presented to the city of Delft by the painter in 1634.

After an adventurous youth, Vroom settled down in Haarlem for a life as an entrepreneur of seascape painting, a specialty of which he was the first professional practitioner. His subject was not the ocean deeps but the coast, usually with recognizable landmarks, and often with identifiable vessels. Many of his works were based on formulas which he filled in with different details. He painted Zandvoort seen from offshore in 1635, for example, in a composition nearly identical to that which he used for a view of Scheveningen twelve years earlier, while his portrayals of the inland ports of Amsterdam, Alkmaar and Haarlem are mutually distinguishable only to those who know the skylines of those cities. Vroom would offer such paintings to the town government, either for sale or as a gift for which he would accept an honorarium in return.

This view of Delft from the north is unusual for the large amount of land in the scene, and for the figures working on it. Otherwise it fits into one of Vroom's schematic types, which was also employed for a view of Veere in Zeeland. We would be inclined to see it as a purely commercial product – albeit an unusually captivating one – were it not for the following document in the Delft archives: 'On June 23, 1634, Master Vroom of Haarlem presented the burgomasters of this city with the portrayal of the city of Delft, painted by his own hand, in regard of the special affection he has always felt for this city, his mother being buried in the Old Church, and the aforesaid Master Vroom having learned his art here in his youth.' By way of thanks, the burgomasters gave the painter 150 guilders.

Bol 1973, p.26.

# Town and country

Painting is a profession for city boys. The fact that Holland was one of the most urbanized countries of Europe in the period with which we are dealing has a lot to do with the vitality of Dutch art, which impressed visitors from all over Europe. In the mid-sixteenth century there were still traces in Holland of earlier, non-urban ways for a painter to make a living: as a monk engaged in the illumination of manuscripts, for example, or as the household retainer of a great lord, responsible for mural decorations and tapestries in castles and palaces. The rejection of the Catholic Church and the decline of the nobility in Holland did not end patronage from these sources, but they did cut the painter loose from patrons who were his legal masters.

The painter as a city shopkeeper is a type we encounter in northern Europe since the early fourteenth century or earlier, but from the mid-sixteenth on, virtually all painters working in Holland complied to this norm, if only from lack of an alternative. Yet it would be a mistake to think of the Dutch painter simply as an independent professional, relying only on his talent and business sense for success in the world. Old patterns of mutual interdependence between painters, along with established and emerging forms of patronage and selling finished works, made it necessary for an artist to find a position within the art world, and build up connections with outside worlds, before he could begin to prosper. Needless to say, this limited one's independence and imposed a certain degree of conformity. This was however not seen as a problem by Dutch artists. The society in which they lived was a meshwork of clans and cults, financial and civic interests, and no one was expected to stand out on his own or break away from the pack. Even excellence in art was perceived as a matter of maintaining standards, or improving incrementally on the work of one's predecessors and contemporaries, rather than electrifying the world with hitherto unknown wonders of technique or style.

The main institution of which a Dutch painter had to take account was the guild. Painters' guilds tended to be named after the patron saint of the profession, St. Luke, who according to legend painted the portrait of Mary with the Christ child. The guilds were organized by town, and each was completely independent of the other, with its own statutes and its own ties to the local government. A well-functioning guild of St. Luke in a Dutch town would protect its members against competition by preventing non-members from selling their work within the town, and by reserving to qualified masters

## 82

JACOB GERRITSZ. CUYP
(1594-1651)
*Michiel Pompe van Slingelandt (1643-1685) at the age of six*. Signed and dated *JCuyp fecit A° 1649*, inscribed *AEtatis 6/1649*. Panel, 106.5 × 78 cm.

The Netherlands Office for Fine Arts, inv.nr.NK 1695 (on loan to Dordrechts Museum). Purchased by the state from the collection of Jonkvrouwe Anna Maria Backer, widow of Abraham Jacob Blaauw, whose father F. de Wildt was a direct descendant of the sitter.

The identity of the sitter was established only in 1982, by A. Kuiper-Ruempel and E. Wolleswinkel. Needless to say, young Michiel comes from a wealthy family. His father Matthijs Pompe was a burgher who became the first Baron of Slingelandt and Capelle, lord of Dordtsmonde, Carnisse, Waelsdorp etc. etc., as well as occupying high offices in the city government of Dordrecht. In 1644, he commissioned a typically burgher family group portrait from Hendrick Martensz. Sorgh in which the family sits in the parlour of their town house, with a view of Dordrecht on the wall behind them. Five years later, it was obviously his position in the gentry that Matthijs

wished to bring out in this portrait of his son. To my eye he and his painter succeeded perfectly in this aim, but carping specialists in falconry have pointed out that the bird on the boy's hand is a kestrel, a type of falcon which has never been used in their royal sport.

Jacob Gerritsz. Cuyp was the leading Dordrecht painter of the day. His own position in Dordrecht society, as deacon and elder of the Walloon Church, was not inconsiderable. His son Aelbert was actually to serve on the high court of South Holland from 1679 to 1682

– not quite as influential an office as those occupied by the young sitter from 1672 on, but one which brought him closer to the social world of his father's patrons than one might have imagined.

Kuiper-Ruempel and Wolleswinkel 1982.

## 83

JACOB VAN DER CROOS
(active 1644-1681)
*View of The Hague, 1663,
with twenty views of spots in
the surroundings, one dated
1661 and seven 1662.* Panel,
64.5 × 123.5 (middle),
17.5 × 32 (surrounding
panels). The places are all
identified in the museum
catalogue.

The Hague, Gemeentemu-
seum, inv.nr. 31ZJ.
Probably purchased by the
burgomasters of The
Hague in 1733 for the
orphans' chamber in the
town hall. Presently on
loan to the town hall.

and

## 84

ANTHONIS JANSZ. VAN
DER CROOS (ca. 1606-after
1662)
*Eik en Duinen (Oak and
Dunes), The Hague.* Panel,
51.5 × 43.5 cm.

The Hague, Gemeentemu-
seum, inv.nr. 14-1922.
Presented to the museum
in 1922 by Jos. H. Gos-
schalk.

One of the twenty motifs
from Jacob van der
Croos's painted tour of the
environs of The Hague
was picked up by his kinsman Anthonis for separate
treatment.

**85**

JAN STEEN (1626-1679)
*The fresh water fish market beside the St. Jacobskerk, The Hague.* Signed and dated 1654. Panel, 59 × 71.5 cm.

The Hague, Gemeentemuseum, inv. nr. 33-26. Acquired in 1926 with the financial aid of the art historian Abraham Bredius.

Jan Steen, a native of Leiden, was one of the founding members of the guild of St. Luke there in 1648. A year later he married the daughter of The Hague landscape painter Jan van Goyen and moved to that nearby town, where he lived until 1654.

**86**

GERRIT ADRIAENSZ.
BERCKHEYDE (1636–1698)
*The Elswout estate in Over-
veen.* Painted in the 1660s.
Panel, 52 × 80 cm.

The Netherlands Office for
Fine Arts, inv. nr. NK 2580
(on loan to Frans Halsmu-
seum, cat. nr. 464b). Seized
by the Germans from the
D. Katz gallery, Dieren.
Formerly in the Cook col-
lection, Richmond.

The owner of Elswout
when this picture was
painted was the Amster-
dam merchant and agent
of the Danish crown
Gabriel Marselis, who
acquired it half-built in

1654 and turned it into one
of the most splendid
country houses in the
Republic. His money
came mainly from the
arms trade. Marselis's
brother Pieter and his
brother-in-law Thomas
Kellerman had an iron
mine and foundry on the
Oka River not far from
Moscow, the products of
which he traded in
Amsterdam. The Marse-
lises operated on the principles of the arms mer-
chant in G.B. Shaw's
*Major Barbara*, who felt
that it was unethical for a
person in his position to
decide who deserved
weapons and who didn't.
The family ethics led them

to smuggle arms to the
Spanish garrison of Ant-
werp when it was under
siege by the French in
alliance with the Republic,
and to other activities
which the historian of the
Amsterdam regents char-
acterized delicately as 'not
exactly fair.' Marselis was
an important patron of the
arts, and Elswout a re-
nowned meeting point for
highly placed art-lovers.
The draughtsman seen
from the back on the left
of the scene will have been
at home there.

Elias 1903–1905, vol. 2,
pp. 871, 875. Exhib. cat. *La
vie en Hollande au XVIIe
siècle*, nr. 47.

**87**

DANIEL VOSMAER (active mid-seventeenth century) *View of Delft from an imaginary palace*. Signed and dated *D. Vosmaer 1663*. Canvas, 90.5 × 113 cm.

The Netherlands Office for Fine Arts, inv.nr.NK 2927 (on loan to the Prinsenhof Museum, Delft). Seized by the Germans from the Goudstikker gallery (see nr.21).

Daniel Vosmaer and his brother Nicolaes are a fascinating but obscure factor in the story of mid-seventeenth century Delft painting. That they were figures of some importance is illustrated by documents concerning a lost work with a deliciously intriguing story.

On June 12, 1666, Daniel Vosmaer appeared before a Delft notary to make a declaration concerning a large painting containing a landscape and a seascape. (Compare nr. 81.) The composition had been sketched in chalk on the support by the late Carel Fabritius, worked up by Daniel in the land sections and his deceased brother Nicolaes in the ships and sea, and then touched up by Fabritius. When it was finished it hung for several years in the town hall, and was now in the Prinsenhof. Since Fabritius was killed in the 1654 explosion (see nr.39), the painting must have been finished at least twelve years previously. Daniel Vosmaer, the only surviving collaborator, declared that he had sold his share of the work, being one-third, to an art dealer named Meynardus de Cooge.

On August 31, two other witnesses declared before a different notary that they had heard Vosmaer say that he had only sold one-fourth of the painting to de Cooge. The testimony was deposed at the request of a third party, Abraham de Potter, who claimed that *he* was the owner of the work. To confuse matters more, in the intervening weeks two Delft artists had testified that in their opinion, Fabritius's share was not worth nearly a third, nor even a fourth. The landscape, they said, which Fabritius hadn't retouched

the right to sign a painting. It would also defend its members against each other by limiting the number of apprentices that a master could take on and fixing a maximum length for the working day and minimum length of training periods, to prevent those with more capital or more energy than the rest from swamping the market. Painters were grateful for these safeguards, but they would have had to be superhuman not to resent the curtailments of entrepreneurial (as opposed to artistic) freedom they brought with them. Another ground for discontent with the guilds was, as we have seen, that they joined artists with housepainters in one organization as wielders of the brush.

Differences between guild structures, and between the ties joining a guild and the local patriciate, were one of the factors behind the division of Dutch art into 'schools' by city. It may not have been a general rule, but one has the impression that a strong or prestigious guild strengthened the forming of a pronounced stylistic image in a certain place at a certain time. Leiden, for example, was for a long time the only large city in the Republic to lack a painters' guild. During that period there was no identifying trait associated with art in Leiden, and most of the best painters, among them Rembrandt and Jan Lievens, abandoned the city for greener pastures elsewhere. It was not until 1648 that a guild was founded, and it was around that time that Leiden painting began to gel into a recognizable style – that of the 'fijnschilders,' the obsessive describers of surface and detail. The conspicuous role played by cloth merchants and their guild in supporting Leiden painting is responsible in part for this development, if only for its commissioning of such paintings as cat.nr. 32. Gerard Dou had been practicing this kind of painting in Leiden for some time by then, but it was not until his influence became manifest in the works of younger masters like van der Tempel, Brekelenkam, Metsu and, especially, Frans van Mieris, that it blossomed into a 'school' that was to live on into the eighteenth century.

Painting in Amsterdam showed the characteristics of stylistic unity only for a brief period in the early seventeenth century, when Pieter Lastman, Jan and Jacob Pynas, Jan Tengnagel and Werner van den Valckert forged a style of history painting that gained recognition throughout the Republic and abroad. Thanks perhaps to Tengnagel, a guild officer and a figure of some political weight in the city, this was the time when the Amsterdam guild of St. Luke was operating at maximum effectiveness. In later years, it was to lose its grip on the teeming art life of Amsterdam, as even the most essential guild provisions fell by the wayside,[1] as did stylistic coherence. Today, if one speaks of the 'Amsterdam school,' it is in reference to the architecture of the 1910s through the '30s, built to strict stylistic specifications.

In the older, smaller and more self-conscious city of Haarlem, cooperation between artists was a matter of course. The artistic life of the city was

at all, was by far the best part of the painting, and was certainly worth fifty guilders more than the seascape.

Even if one or more of the declarations is what is known in the art of negotiating as a smoke screen, the affair still has the makings of an equation with one unknown too many. Still, it is a great pity we know no more about it. Two interesting things it does teach us are that a single painting could be a joint venture both artistically and financially; and that Daniel Vosmaer collaborated on a major work with the most talented Delft painter of his time, Fabritius. For the painting, see the text.

Brown 1981, pp. 154-156.

**88**

NICOLAES VERKOLJE
(1673-1746)
*David van Mollem (1670-1746) and his family*. Signed and dated *Verkolje 1740*.
Panel, 63.5 × 79 cm.

The Netherlands Office for Fine arts, inv.nr.C 1882 (on loan to Amsterdams Historisch Museum, cat.nr.472, inv.nr.B 5728)

The painting was one of the centrepieces of an excellent exhibition of 1981 dedicated to the house and silk factory in which this scene takes place, an estate called Zijdebalen (Silk Bales) on the Vecht River between Utrecht and Maarssen. The authors of the catalogue traced the history of the van Mollem family silk business from the mid-seventeenth century until its sad end in 1816. The high point of the history was formed by the career of David van Mollem, who built Zijdebalen. We see him here in a painting that was probably made on the occasion of his seventieth birthday, a proud pater familias in an environment of his own making, surrounded by his progeny.

Van Mollem was a Mennonite, and he dressed in the plain black that was prescribed for all adherents of that faith. Opposite him sits his daughter-in-law Maria van Oosterwijk (not the still-life painter of that name), clad gloriously in the silks which made the van Mollems rich. All the details of the painting are moralized. Even the mulberry bush with its silkworms in the middle of the terrace is not left to speak for itself: on the edge of the pot in which it stands we read the motto 'In esca lubrum' (Profit through eating). One can practically hear old van Mollem pinning the appropriate moral on everything and everybody in his ken, just as in the painting he is pointing out to his grandson David a print of the Good Samaritan with the legend 'Hac

dominated by a succession of major figures: between 1580 and 1630. Cornelis Cornelisz. van Haarlem, Hendrick Goltzius, Frans Hals, and Frans de Grebber, each in his turn, provided a focus for the intellectual and artistic energies of the more talented Haarlem artists. The studios and personal influence of these figures seem to have made up for the lack of a strong guild for the half-century following iconoclasm. Their authority was backed up by the long tradition of Haarlem painting and art training. Carel van Mander was a Haarlemer, and proud of it, when he wrote his *Painter's book*, the Bible of the Dutch artist for the seventeenth century. However, intellectual distinction and personal ascendancy are not synonymous with good organization, and in 1630 the city demanded that the artists of Haarlem put their house in order and reform the guild. In their reaction, they 'attempted to give the traditional guild a new meaning by building the academic mode of training into the guild structure. This ... casts new light on the work of the painters generally known as the Haarlem classicists, who are finally beginning to attract some admiring attention from scholars,' as the Dutch art historian Ed Taverne observed fourteen years ago.[2] The classicism to which he referred is best embodied in the exhibition in cat.nr.22, by a painter who belonged to a branch of the Haarlem school in Amersfoort.

In Utrecht too the fortunes of the guild rose and fell concurrently with the city's image as an art centre with a style of its own. It was not until 1611 that the painters were allowed to form a guild of St. Luke, after having been encumbered with an undesired association with the saddlers since the middle ages. Until 1639 the guild operated in the traditional way, at which point the artist-painters split off into a College of Painters which, however, never attained the same authority as the guild. Between 1611 and 1639, the Utrecht school of painting was at its height, projecting an image of Italianate modernity that put it in the forefront of the Dutch art world. The leading figure for much of that period was Paulus Moreelse, dean of the guild and member of the Utrecht town council.

There was not always a guild or a magnetic individual behind the emergence of a local school. Delft began to take on the glamour of a major centre towards the mid-seventeenth century for no observable reason. Starting then, Delft shone for two decades, establishing its eternal reputation for church paintings, architectural views (cat.nr.87) and of course for the work of Vermeer. Before and after, Delft lacked anything coming close to that concentrated glow, and was just another town where a certain number of painters worked. An original theory explaining the sudden emergence of Delft has been proposed by Walter Liedtke: 'Until 1650, the art of this profoundly conservative, patriotic, provincial town was cultivated in the light and shade of the court. The Hague is about six miles away, and the palaces at Rijswijk and Honselaarsdijk were

itur in caelum via' (This is the way to get to heaven). On the back of the painting, for good measure, is painted the family tree of the sitters, in the form of a mulberry bush.

To create an environment like Zijdebalen, one has to be a practiced patron of the arts, aware of what a particular artist can and cannot do. Van Mollem, obviously, was that kind of person. One cannot help wondering whether his star might not have shined more brilliantly than it did if he had been a little less well organized and sure of himself.

Exhib. cat. *Zijdebalen.*

**89**

HENDRIK POTHOVEN
(1725-1795)
*Stadholder Willem V and his family at the kermis on the Buitenhof.* Signed and dated 1781. Panel, 61 × 85 cm.

The Hague, Gemeente-museum, inv.nr. 34-26. Acquired in 1926.

In early May, every year from 1407 to 1885, the area around the Buitenhof in The Hague was transformed into a grounds for the court fair or *hofkermis*, the greatest event of its kind in the country. For the duration of the kermis a special freedom prevailed which was relished by everyone in the town. In earlier centuries the freedom was regulated by custom or even law: guilds relaxed their prohibitions, the sheriff's men looked the other way when feuds were fought out, the church gave unmarried young lovers its blessing. Artists traditionally took advantage of the kermis to sell their works from stalls in the streets to visiting outsiders.

By the late eighteenth century, the kermis had taken on manners, although Pothoven's depiction of it strikes us as a bit too well-behaved to be believed. The presence of the stadholder and his family would have quieted things down a bit but not all that much: their informal visits were a traditional part of the celebration. In the seventeenth century, as stadholder, Willem III would review the civic guard which paraded past his quarter of the inner court (the building on the right) and then go out in the streets with his Mary to buy presents. In a later year, as King William III of England, he once said that he would give 'a hundred, nay two hundred thousand guilders to be able to fly like a bird to the Hague kermis.' (Today a flight would not cost him much more than one-thousandth that amount.)

One report of a nineteenth-century royal visit to the kermis mentions that at the end of the festive day a ball was held at the court, at which a lottery was held with paintings and other works of art as prizes, including objects which had been bought at the kermis. Pothoven's painting is too precious to have been raffled off that way, but it may well have served as a souvenir for someone.

As it happens, the ker-

closer still... But after the unexpected death of Willem II in November 1650, and the sudden rise of Amsterdam (already the commercial capital) as the political and social center of the Netherlands, painters in Delft turned from the taste of the court to everything the more northern schools had achieved.... This artistic milieu embraced the early work of Vermeer, the arrival of Paulus Potter and Carel Fabritius from Amsterdam and of Pieter de Hooch from Haarlem, and architectural painting in Delft.'[3] Perhaps it was chance that, as Michael Montias adds, 'these innovative "foreigners," together with their Delft-based colleagues,... shared a sensibility to the effects of light and air and an interest in space construction and perspective... A genuine school – in the sense of a community with intersecting interests in subject matter and techniques, with some similarity in aesthetic approaches, and with significant cross-influences – had at last come into existence. But a critical mass, in the sense of a number of individuals large enough to preserve the intensity of interaction necessary to keep a community of artists from drifting apart, is sooner lost than won. When a community is small to begin with, it only takes a few deaths or departures for it to disintegrate.'[4]

mis of 1781 was the last one at which a stadholder of the Republic could relax with his family among a Dutch crowd. On September 26th of that year, a pamphlet entitled *To the Netherlands people* gave the impulse to a revolutionary movement that was not to abate until Willem was driven out of the country on January 18, 1795. (See nr. 52). It is something of an historical wonder that in 1815 a prince of Orange once more ruled the country, as King Willem I. We see him here, on the eve of the great cataclysm, as the nine-year-old son of the last stadholder.

Van Gelder 1937. Pippel 1941, pp.137-148. Schama 1977, p.64.

Some of the smaller centres we have discussed – Leiden, Utrecht and Delft – profited greatly in the course of the centuries from their association in the mind of the art-loving public with a single, well-defined style. Along with Leiden woolens, velours d'Utrecht and Delftware, the local schools of painting served to distinguish these cities in the mind of large groups of people all over the world. Centres such as The Hague and Dordrecht, which also supported communities of painters, but which were not blessed with a visual trademark, a stylistic slogan, are at a disadvantage by comparison. The Hague had to wait for two centuries for its 'school,' and Dordrecht is waiting still.

The emergence of a characteristic local school, it seems safe to say, is less a function of regionalism than of particularism. Naturally there are deep issues involved. The old ties of Utrecht to Rome, for example, certainly influenced the form taken by painting in Utrecht; the Leiden commitment to the cloth industry was not without its effect on the appeal of Dou and van Mieris; the fame of the Delft churches, especially the Old Church, with the tomb of the House of Orange, drew the painters of the city towards architecture. But every city has peculiarities of this kind, and in few do they take shape in an artistic style. When we look at the circumstances which led to the emergence of the successful schools, we are guided towards interests of a more short-lived and mundane nature. A group of artists with a stake in a local party – the guild of St. Luke, the traders in some particular product such as say or wool, a faction in the town council, a prominent clan with an interest in art – will discover that they are producing art that is recognizable to their patrons and others as a school. If their work is also commercially successful, it will attract followers and consolidate into a current. If it burns with a white heat, at the right place and time, the phenomenon does not have to endure for very long in order to become everlastingly famous.

No town without country. If there was one specialty that attracted all those city-boy painters more than another, it was landscape. In Delft, where Michael Montias has analyzed the subjects of nearly ten thousand paintings mentioned in probate inventories between 1610 and 1679, twenty-five percent of all the paintings at the beginning of that period, and more than forty percent at the end, were pure landscapes. If we add to these a portion of the religious and secular histories and battle scenes, many of which are located on the land, we come to the amazing conclusion that nearly half the late seventeenth-century Dutch paintings were landscapes![5]

The taste for the countryside in art kept pace with the urge to the outdoors that captivated the Dutch middle and upper classes from the early seventeenth century on. All over the Republic, those who could afford it were renting or buying space from landowners for everything ranging from weekend accommodations on a patch of ground to complete country estates. In the present author's own town of Maarssen, this process was accomplished between 1610 and 1660, and was completely arranged by one Amsterdam burgomaster's family, the Huydecopers. They bought up the best riverside properties in Maarssen, had themselves dubbed Lords of Maarsseveen, built splendid country houses for themselves and their Amsterdam kinsmen where simple farms had stood, drove the original inhabitants back into the soggy hinterland, brought in poets to describe the joys of the bucolic life – in short, turned a piece of Dutch countryside into an attribute of a wealthy city clan.[6] Once this had been done, Maarssen became an interesting object for artists. Before the Huydecoper campaign, no artist is known to have expended his talents on the place. But from mid-century on, the houses and landscape of the town and its surroundings were immortalized in drawings by Antonie Waterlo,[7] in prints by Roelant Roghman and in paintings by Jan van der Heyden – all Amsterdamers, from the bailiwick of the Huydecopers. Their portrayals of country houses and landscape would go back to the city, of course.

The tie between town and country is visible in the 1635 view of Delft by Hendrick Vroom (cat.nr.81), where the churches of Delft and the canal linking Delft to The Hague dominate the scene. Daniel Vosmaer's 1663 panorama of the city (cat.nr.87) may not look it, but it too is a paean to country life. The imaginary palace from which the view is painted is located outside the walls of Delft, on the far end of a line from the New Church through the two windmills we see on the right of Vroom's painting. City folk with more of a

**90**

PAUL CONSTANTIJN LA
FARGUE (1729–1782)
*The Groenmarkt, The
Hague.* Panel, 57 × 76 cm.

Neither the street scene
nor the painterly con-
ception of this painting is
very different from those
of Jan Steen's view of a
century earlier (cat.nr. 85).

**91**

WILLEM BARTEL VAN
DER KOOI (1768-1836)
*A father's joy.* Signed and
dated *W.B. van der Kooi,
faciebat 1816.* Canvas,
101 × 111 cm.

Leeuwarden, Fries
Museum, inv.nr. 1948-73
(on loan from Museum
Boymans-van Beuningen,
which acquired it by
bequest from L.V. Lede-
boer Bz. in 1891, with the
following entry).

Academic prizes for excellent young scholars were
instituted under the French
in 1806. The artist himself
was the beneficiary of
more substantial rewards
during that period, both
academic and political. A
radical Patriot, he served as
secretary of the Frisian
county of Achtkarspelen
from 1795 to 1800, and
from 1798 to 1811 was
Lecturer in Drawing at the
Franeker Academy. Van
der Kooi used his political
position, and took personal
initiatives, to save local
works of art – the tombs
of the Nassau stadholders
of Friesland and church
altarpieces – from icono-
clastic depradation.

The choice of subject
may not have been van der
Kooi's. *A father's joy* was
commissioned in 1816,
years after the artist had
stopped painting scenes of
everyday life, by the
Amsterdam collector S.M.
de Boer, who had a special
attachment to Friesland.

Boschma 1978, cat.nr. E
249.

**92**

WILLEM BARTEL VAN
DER KOOI (1768-1836)
*A mother's joy*. Signed and
dated *W.B. van der Kooi /
faciebat 1818*. Canvas,
102 × 113 cm.

Leeuwarden, Fries
Museum, inv.nr. 1948-72
(on loan from Museum
Boymans-van Beuningen,
Rotterdam, which
acquired it in the same
way as the preceding
entry).

This painting, like the
preceding one, has also
been brought into con-
nection with French ideals
of raising children. Until
the publication of Jean-
Jacques Rousseau's novel
*Emile* in 1762, sophisticated
French mothers avoided
giving the breast to their
babies. Rousseau's
influence helped bring the
practice into fashion in
those circles. Although in
the Netherlands mothers

had never stopped breast-
feeding their infants, those
who subscribed to Rous-
seau's notions of natural
education could now do so
with ideological con-
viction. The manner in
which this young mother
shows an older child how
she gives the breast can
itself be interpreted as an
application of 'natural'
education.

The outspokenly pro-
vincial garb of the figures

may have been intended
by artist and patron to
express not just local custom but also the somewhat
smug message that plain
Frisian mothers were in
the possession of truths
that French intellectuals
had to rediscover with
great effort. However, in
1818 there was nothing
plain about van der Kooi
or his Amsterdam patron.

Boschma 1978, cat.nr.251.

**93**

BARTHOLOMEUS
JOHANNES VAN HOVE
(1790–1880)
*The garden of Gedempte
Burgwal 34, The Hague,
with a view of the Paviljoen-
gracht.* Signed and dated
*B.J. van Hove 1828.* Canvas, 82 × 66.5 cm.

The Hague, Gemeentemu-
seum, inv. nr. 229.

We are all familiar with
paintings of Dutch inte-
riors in which a landscape
hangs on the wall. Here
we see a reversal of that
image: a garden with a
framed view of a city
canal. The effect is magical. Van Hove was the son

of a framemaker, and was
trained in that profession
before going into painting.
The interior framing in
this composition betrays
the influence of his old
profession. He used the
same device to great effect
in his stage backdrop for
*The siege of Leiden* a few
years later, in which the
townscape is seen from a
garden in the foreground.
In 1833 van Hove was
honoured with a medal
and a rich order for paintings by Tsar Nicholas I of
Russia, and he was the
drawing teacher of Nicho-
las's sister Anna Paulowna,
daughter of Paul I and
consort of King Willem II
of the Netherlands. For

Willem as well, who
mounted the throne in
1840, van Hove painted his
palace and garden in The
Hague. This painting can
be seen as a bourgeois pre-
decessor of the civic and
royal commissions in van
Hove's future. The iden-
tity of the owner of the
garden is unfortunately
not mentioned in the
literature on the painting.

Immerzeel 1842, vol. 2,
pp. 59-60. Bol 1965.

Fig. 8
J.H. Weissenbruch,
*Bleaching fields,* dated 1847.
Canvas, 40 × 60 cm. The
Hague, Gemeente-
museum.

feeling for natural landscape will be sooner attracted to the twenty views of places in the outskirts of The Hague (cat.nr. 83), which however are plainly presented as belonging to the city which shines in their midst – pleasant afternoon walks for the office slave with a day off. The painting now hangs in the town hall of The Hague, which has long since gobbled up most of the places portrayed. Oak and Dunes, which provides the motif of a separate view (cat.nr. 84), has escaped being asphalted only because it has become a cemetery.

No town without the produce of the country, either. The fresh water fish being sold in the square in The Hague in Jan Steen's painting (cat.nr. 85) was caught in the surrounding countryside, the vegetables in La Fargue's market scene (cat.nr. 90) grown there. The farmers would come into town on market days with their wares, and return with city goods, which included many paintings. According to the well-known account of the Englishman John Evelyn, who visited Holland in 1641, the fairs were full of paintings, 'especially Landscips, and Drolleries, as they call those clownish representations. The reason of this store of pictures and their cheapenesse proceede from their want of Land, to employ their Stock; so as 'tis an ordinary thing to find, a common Farmor lay out two, or 3000 pounds in this Commodity, their houses are full of them, and they vend them at their Kermas'es to very great gaines.'[8] The farmer was therefore not only a consumer but actually a dealer in art. It is astonishing to think that as many as a third of the Dutch paintings of the Golden Age may have been created as a form of capital investment for farmers with more money than land.

The market for landscapes, the most massive and seemingly the most impersonal segment of the Dutch world of painting, may have been closer to the bone than any other. It was at those kermis booths where turnips shared space with paintings that the artist's vision came most fully into its own. There he could turn the figments of his imagination into food for his family, while down-to-earth farmers could appease their hunger for land with painted substitutes, dreams of landscape as scrip held against hopes of farmland in the future.

1. Haak 1984, p. 31.
2. Taverne 1972-1973, p. 66.
3. Liedtke 1982, p. 11.
4. Montias 1982, p. 181.
5. Montias 1982, p. 242.
6. Schwartz 1973.
7. Broos 1984.
8. Quoted in Rosenberg, Slive and ter Kuile 1966, p. 9.

Fig. 9
Vincent van Gogh, *Head of a young peasant with a pipe*. Painted in 1885. Canvas laid down on panel, 38 × 30 cm. Amsterdam, Rijksmuseum Vincent van Gogh (Vincent van Gogh Foundation).

# The invisible world

In the preceding chapters, we have traced the connections between Dutch artists and their fellow countrymen in all areas of society, from burgomasters and cloth merchants ordering decorations for splendid new buildings, to a banker having a proud professional memory immortalized, to farmers buying landscape paintings when they could not invest in land. The emphasis has been on the material values that artists shared with their public, on art as an integral feature of social, business and political life.

To some degree, this emphasis is intended as a corrective to the prevailing view of art as a primarily spiritual activity. In our day, artists are still widely regarded as visionaries who see further than the burgher, as prophetic creatures responsible only to their own creative genius. The painters of Holland in most of the period covered by the exhibition enjoyed no such special status. The highest praise a painter could expect in this regard is that he was intelligent enough to understand someone else's text or idea, and skilled enough to depict it accurately in paint.

If Dutch painting was not expected by its original audience to be filled with profundity, neither was it dismissed as superficial. In the older tradition of sacred art from which modern painting developed, the painter *was* the bearer of a deep message – not a personal one, but that of God and the church. With the rejection by Calvinism of art as a tool of worship, Dutch painters found themselves in the position of the atheist being buried in a tuxedo: all dressed up and no place to go.

It took a few decades, but eventually they did find a place to go. Without offending Calvinist sensibilities, some Dutch painters yet found a way to give expression to the religious values which had in the past brought so much honour to their profession. The solution was cast in metaphorical terms by the merchant-poet Roemer Visscher, in a book of emblems he brought out in 1614. The first emblem – a motto with an illustration and a caption – shows 'a hand pushing an empty flask or glass bottle into the water, with the mouth turned down; nonetheless, the flask does not fill with water, because it is full of compressed air. Which is intended to signify that, although it may not be apparent, God fills everything.'

That insight took shape in Dutch art in a characteristic way. Traditional devotional imagery gave way to pictures of everyday objects and scenes which, 'although it may not be apparent,' were filled with spiritual messages. They

**94**

HENDRICK GERRITSZ.
POT (ca. 1585-1657)
*Allegory of transitoriness.*
Painted in the 1620s?
Panel, 58 × 73 cm.

The Netherlands Office for
Fine Arts, inv.nr.NK 2589
(on loan to Frans Halsmu-
seum, cat.nr.469a)

Eddy de Jongh has demon-
strated the ties between
this painting and a print by
Jacques de Gheyn II,
where the old woman is
herself a skeleton and the

message is laid on that
much more thickly: what
good is your wealth when
death knocks at the door?

Jacques de Gheyn was a
court artist to the stadholder, Prince Maurits. Hen-
drick Pot, a Haarlem mas-
ter of high social standing,
must also have had ties to
the court. In 1620 the
town of Haarlem paid him
450 Flemish pounds for a
monumental allegorical
painting of *The apotheosis
of William the Silent*,
Maurits's father, for the
Prinsenhof. In the 1630s,

Pot spent a period of time
at the court of King
Charles I of England,
which may be taken as a
sign that he was in favour
with the Dutch stadholder
as well.

The combination of
princely praise, sexual imagery and warnings of the
nearness of death may
seem strange at first
glance, but it made sense at
the court of the Calvinist
generalissimo Maurits.
Remember too that other
painting that the town of
Haarlem ordered for the

Prinsenhof, where Maurits
stayed on his visits to the
city: *A monk squeezing the
breast of a nun* (cat.nr.11).

Exhib. cat. *Tot lering en
vermaak*, nr.52. Exhib. cat.
*Prijst de lijst*, nr.8.

were also filled with closely observed details of the natural and social worlds, depicted with artistry and loving care. One of the most exciting developments in Dutch art history in our time is the rediscovery and interpretation of those messages. Many of the still-life and genre paintings which for centuries were regarded as straightforward registrations of reality have been shown to contain moral meanings.

The technique of doing this, and the idea behind it, were not invented in the seventeenth century. Since the middle ages, artists had been investing the objects and figures in sacred art with deeper meanings. However, those objects and figures were formerly details in paintings of standard religious subjects. The main significance of the scene – and God's presence in it – was immediately apparent. With the elimination of a recognizably religious subject, the viewer had to know beforehand what the artist intended to convey before he could understand it. And even then... One of Roemer Visscher's other emblems in the same book shows the sun and the wind exerting themselves to penetrate the glass window of a 'church or house.' The sun succeeds and the wind fails. 'This requires no further explanation,' says Visscher. 'Everyone can use it anyway it suits him.' A good image, in other words, is not to be scorned, even if it doesn't mean anything in particular. A viewer who likes it will come up with a meaning easily enough.

The paintings in this section of the exhibition contain images of that kind. Images pregnant with a content that threatens to escape us, but which will not let us go. We would like to interpret them according to their makers' intention, but we have the unhappy suspicion that if the makers were alive to be interrogated, they would tell us to interpret them any way we like. I have called them images of the invisible world, for they deal with things unseen, like thoughts, feelings and sounds.

The two examples from the first half of the seventeenth century, by Hendrick Pot and Jan van Bijlert, are the most traditional. They evoke the biblical but nearly anti-religious saying of Solomon's, 'Vanity of vanities, all is vanity.' The young woman reading a letter we know is a love letter (cat.nr.94), turning her jewel-cases and hatboxes inside out to dress for what we know is a tryst, a tryst which, we thrill to think with her, might end in the curtained bed, has a death's-head held up to her by the crone who attends on her. She is not impressed. The grinding mills of the gods, which kill us all anyway sooner or later, cannot keep up with her pulse.

The beautiful young woman with the kerchief tucked loosely between her breasts holds up her own reminder of death, a ticking watch. She looks into the mirror, where she can also see the reflection of the angelic child holding a blown-out candle. Has time already run out on her? Jan van Bijlert, we recall, was on the board of a hospital for syphilitics. Can the message of his painting be

**95**

JAN VAN BIJLERT
(1597–1671)
*Anna Grave(?): allegory of transitoriness.* Signed *J. v. Bijlert ft.* Painted in the 1630s? Canvas, 76×88.5 cm.

The Netherlands Office for Fine Arts, inv.nr.c 1869. Presented in 1967 by A.H. van der Mersch, Zeist.

On the back of the panel is the inscription, in Dutch: Anna Grave, daughter of Hendrik and Maria van ...,

first married August 13, 1656 to Hendrik Verbeek and remarried to Mr. Cornelis Sijdervelt of Arnemuiden, Zeeland. She died on January 23, 1680 and was the grandmother of Maria Sijdervelt, who married Pieter van der Mersch, lord of Zuidland and Volkersdijk, born in 1702.

The families concerned were closely related to the Mennonite van Mollems (see cat.nr.88), who also had a penchant for moral allegory. Knowing the

family manners, we find it hard to believe that a young matron of this line would have herself painted as an example of how not to behave in life. It seems more likely that the painting was not a portrait, but that once it had become a family heirloom, later owners tried to identify the woman as one of their ancestors.

For the painter, see Bok 1984, pp.31-34.

**96**

EMANUEL DE WITTE
(1618–1692)
*Interior with a woman playing the clavecin to a man in bed*. Painted in the 1660s? Canvas, 77.5 × 104.5 cm.

The Netherlands Office for Fine Arts, inv.nr.NK 2685; seized by the Germans from the collection of Otto Lanz, Amsterdam, 1941. On loan to Museum Boymans-van Beuningen, Rotterdam, inv.nr.2313.

De Jongh sees in this painting a demonstration of the healing power of music. An officer tortured by pain – the pain of love – is forced to take to bed in the middle of the day, hoping that the sweet strains of the clavecin will bring him relief. This may be accurate, but it is not an adequate interpretation of the subdued eroticism in the painting, as de Jongh too admits.

What has always fascinated me about the painting is its visual rhythm. A

view into depth – what the Dutch call a *doorkijkje*, a look from one space into another – is punctuated by grouped strokes of light admitted through large and small windows on the right. They fall on floors which have their own pattern, formed by tiles and floorboards. Squinted at sideways, the light looks like musical notation, evoking the sounds that begin in the front room and carry into the back of the house and beyond. A sense of harmony is cre-

ated between interior space and the outside world.

Houbraken, vol.1, p.282. Exhib. cat. *Tot lering en vermaak*, nr.76.

**97**

NICOLAES MAES (1634-
1693)
*The eavesdropper*. Signed
and dated 1657. Canvas,
92.5 × 122 cm.

The Netherlands Office for
Fine Arts, inv.nr. NK 2560
(on loan to Dordrechts
Museum).

Here too a mystery is
being depicted. Beneath
the carved head of Juno,
the goddess of marriage
and the household, a
young woman cautions us
to be quiet and listen. Her

position in the painting
makes her a binding figure
between the established
household at the table
upstairs and the young
lovers downstairs. The
wild sexual attraction
between youngsters who
think they invented love is
about to set into the
cement of a bourgeois
marriage. What they are
brewing in secret in the
kitchen will later be served
up in public in the dining
room. All to the amuse-
ment of the knowing
eavesdropper who has seen
this happen so many times

before. We are drawn into
a conspiracy of silence by
her gesture.

The scene bears a strik-
ing resemblance to one
sketched by Laurence
Sterne in *Tristram Shandy*,
which I print here for
fellow lovers of that book:
'My mother was going
very gingerly in the dark
along the passage which
led to the parlour, as my
uncle *Toby* pronounced
the word *wife*. – 'Tis a
shrill, penetrating sound of
itself, and *Obadiah* had
helped it by leaving the
door a little a-jar, so that

my mother heard enough
of it, to imagine herself the
subject of the conversa-
tion: so laying the edge of
her finger across her two
lips—holding in her
breath, and bending her
head a little downwards,
with a twist of her neck
—(not towards the door,
but from it, by which
means her ear was brought
to the chink)—she listened
with all her powers:—the
listening slave, with the
Goddess of Silence at his
back, could not have given
a finer thought for an
intaglio.' Or for a Dutch
picture.

156

as cruel as that? Or is it just a warning? If so, it is at least as cruel, to cast temptation in such irresistible guise.

The tension between the sensual and the moral aspects of Dutch painting, which reaches its peak in paintings such as this, is one of the secrets of its appeal. It is also the occasion for periodical disputes in the scholarly world such as the one we are currently enjoying, between Eddy de Jongh of Utrecht University, the pioneer explorer of emblematic and moral meanings of Dutch painting, and Svetlana Alpers of the University of California at Berkeley, who named her provocative book on Dutch seventeenth-century painting *The art of describing*.

In a way, the issue that divides them is inherent in serious art of all kinds. It is not easy to put an earnest message into aesthetically appealing form without compromise. Constantijn Huygens, writing about the poet's attempt to compose uplifting yet palatable poetry, rhymed:

He aims to edify and make it seem a treat.
One reader sniffs the gravy while another chews the meat.
He's satisfied them both, but each with half a serving.

Nonetheless, it seems to me that de Jongh has digested his half-portion better than Alpers hers. He demonstrates beyond doubt that careful thought was devoted to the imagery in many Dutch paintings of everyday life, and he often succeeds, in his all too inimitable style, in approximating the chain of thought behind a particular picture. Alpers seeks to interpret more diffuse aspects of painting (two of her chapters are devoted to 'the nature of picturing in the north' and 'the mapping impulse'), aspects which were not the subject of conscious consideration in the seventeenth century, and certainly were not on the minds of working artists. Predictably, she ends up with diffuse conclusions, and seldom pins down precise meanings, whether of individual paintings or of elements of the Dutch 'visual culture' she set out to study. In writing this catalogue, I nonetheless profited from her work in the field, through several excellent dissertations she inspired and supervised, a contribution I hold in high regard.

The two evocations of the invisible world from the latter half of the seventeenth century (cat.nrs.96, 97) are more complex in construction and more subtle in conception than the earlier examples. Their sexual vibration does not throb, it resonates quietly. The keyboard music we cannot hear is also being listened to by a man we can barely see, the officer in what we presume is the lady's bed. The most beguiling message of all is that being expressed to us by Nicolaes Maes's lady on the stairs. She looks at us and holds her finger to her lips, as if to say: 'If only you would be quiet, you would be able to hear what is going on in this painting.'

*The life and opinions of Tristram Shandy, gentleman,* in eleven volumes, London (Tonson) 1771, vol. 5, chap. 5, p. 202. Exhib. cat. *Tot lering en vermaak,* cat. nr. 34.

# Literature

DE BALBIAN VERSTER 1932
J. F. L. de Balbian Verster, 'Gerard Hulft (1621-1656),' *Jaarboek Amstelodamum* 29 (1932), pp. 131-158

BARBOUR 1963
Violet Barbour, *Capitalism in Amsterdam in the seventeenth century*, Ann Arbor, Michigan (University of Michigan Press) 1963 (first published in 1950 by Johns Hopkins University Press)

DE BAVO TE BOEK 1985
*De Bavo te boek: bij het gereedkomen van de restauratie van de Grote- of St.-Bavo kerk te Haarlem*, Haarlem 1985

BIESBOER 1983
P. Biesboer, *Schilderijen voor het stadhuis Haarlem: zestiende en zeventiende eeuw kunstopdrachten ter verfraaiing*, Haarlem 1983

BILDERS 1974
Gerard Bilders, *Vrolijk versterven: een keuze uit zijn dagboeken en brieven*, ed. Wim Zaal, Amsterdam 1974

BILLE 1961
Clara Bille, *De Tempel de Kunst of het Kabinet van den Heer Braamcamp*, 2 vols., Amsterdam 1961

BLOCH 1949
Vitale Bloch, 'Orlando,' *Oud-Holland* 64 (1949), pp. 104-108

BOK 1984
Marten Jan Bok, *Vijfendertig Utrechtse kunstenaars en hun werk voor het Sint Jobs Gasthuis, 1622-1642*, Utrecht 1984

BOL 1965
L. J. Bol, 'Bartholomeus Johannes van der Hove (1790-1880): *Gezicht vanuit de tuin van Gedempte Burgwal 34, Den Haag*,' *Openbaar Kunstbezit* 9 (1965), nr. 13

BOL 1973
L. J. Bol, *Die holländische Marinemaler des 17. Jahrhunderts*, Braunschweig 1973

BOSCHMA 1978
C. Boschma, *Willem Bartel van der Kooi (1768-1836) en het tekenonderwijs in Friesland*, Leeuwarden 1978

BOXER 1965
C. R. Boxer, *The Dutch sea-borne empire, 1600-1800*, London (Hutchinson) 1965

BREDIUS 1915-1921
A. Bredius, *Künstler-Inventare: Urkunden zur Geschichte der holländischen Kunst des XVIten, XVIIten und XVIIIten Jahrhunderts*, 7 vols., The Hague 1915-1921

BREDIUS AND MOES 1891-1892
A. Bredius and E. W. Moes, 'De schildersfamilie Ravensteyn,' *Oud-Holland* 9 (1891), pp. 204-219, and vol. 10 (1892), pp. 41-52.

BRENNINKMEYER-DE ROOIJ 1977
Beatrijs Brenninkmeyer-de Rooij, 'De schilderijengalerij van Prins Willem V op het Buitenhof te Den Haag (2),' *Antiek* 11 (1977), pp. 138-176

BROOS 1984
Ben P. J. Broos, ''Antoni Waterlo f(ecit)' in Maarsseveen,' *Jaarboekje 1984 van het Oudheidkundige Genootschap 'Niftarlake,'* pp. 18-48

BROWN 1981
Christopher Brown, *Carel Fabritius: complete edition with a catalogue raisonné*, Oxford 1981, pp. 154-156

DE BRUYN KOPS 1964
C. J. de Bruyn Kops, 'Kaspar Karsen (1810-1896), *De Oude Beurs in Amsterdam*,' *Openbaar Kunstbezit* 27 (1964), nr. 8

CAT. AMSTERDAMS HISTORISCH MUSEUM 1975/1979
Albert Blankert, cat. *Schilderijen daterend van voor 1800: voorlopige catalogus*, met bijdragen van Rob Ruurs, Amsterdam (Amsterdams Historisch Museum) 1975/1979

CAT. DE LAKENHAL 1983
(M. L. Wurfbain), *Catalogus van de schilderijen en tekeningen*, Leiden (Stedelijk Museum De Lakenhal) 1983

CAT. MAURITSHUIS 1977
*Illustrated general catalogue*, The Hague (Mauritshuis: The Royal Cabinet of Painting) 1977

DUDOK VAN HEEL 1976
S. A. C. Dudok van Heel, 'De schilder Claes Moyaert en zijn familie,' *Jaarboek Amstelodamum* 68 (1976), pp. 13-48

DUKER 1897-1915
A. C. Duker, *Gisbertus Voetius*, 3 vols., Leiden 1897-1915

VAN EEGHEN 1971
I. H. van Eeghen, 'De vaandeldrager van Rembrandt,' *Maandblad Amstelodamum* 58 (1971), pp. 173-181

VAN EIJNDEN AND VAN DER WILLIGEN
Roeland van Eijnden and Adriaan van der Willigen, *Geschiedenis der vaderlandsche schilderkunst*, 4 vols., Amsterdam 1842

EKKART 1974
R. E. O. Ekkart, 'Leidse schilders, tekenaars en graveurs uit de tweede helft van de 16de en het begin van de 17de eeuw,' *Jaarboekje voor Geschiedenis en Oudheidkunde van Leiden en omstreken* 66 (1974), pp. 171-196

EKKART 1977
R. E. O. Ekkart, *Franeker professorenportretten: iconografie van de professoren aan de Academie en het Rijksathenaeum te Franeker, 1585-1843*, Franeker 1977

EKKART 1978-1979
R. E. O. Ekkart, 'De familiekroniek van Heemskerck en van Swanenburg,' *Jaarboek voor het Centraal Bureau voor Genealogie en het Iconografisch Bureau* 32 (1978), pp. 41-70 and 33 (1979), pp. 44-74

ELIAS 1903-1905
Johan E. Elias, *De vroedschap van Amsterdam, 1578-1795*, 2 vols., Haarlem 1903-1905

EXHIB. CAT. GOD EN DE GODEN
Exhib. cat. *God en de goden* (English: *Gods, saints and heroes*), Washington (National Gallery of Art), Detroit (Institute of Arts) and Amsterdam (Rijksmuseum)

EXHIB. CAT. TOT LERING EN VERMAAK
(E. de Jongh et al.), exhib. cat. *Tot lering en vermaak*, Amsterdam (Rijksmuseum) 1976

EXHIB. CAT. MALER UND MODELL 1979
Exhib. cat. *Maler und Modell*, Baden-Baden (Staatliche Kunsthalle) 1969

EXHIB. CAT. PIETER JANSZ. SAENREDAM
Exhib. cat. *Pieter Jansz. Saenredam*, Utrecht (Centraal Museum) 1961

EXHIB. CAT. HET VADERLANDSCH GEVOEL
Exhib. cat. *Het vaderlandsch gevoel: vergeten negentiende-eeuwse schilderijen over onze geschiedenis*, Amsterdam (Rijksmuseum) 1978

EXHIB. CAT. LA VIE EN HOLLANDE
Exhib. cat. *La vie en Hollande au XVIIe siècle: tableaux, dessins, estampes, argenterie, monnaies, médailles et autres témoignages*, Paris (Musée des Arts Decoratifs, organisée par l'Institut Néerlandais) 1967

EXHIB. CAT. ZIJDEBALEN
Exhib. cat. *Zijdebalen – Lusthof aan de Vecht: tuin- en tekenkunst uit het begin van de achttiende eeuw*, Utrecht (Centraal Museum) 1981

FREEDBERG 1985
David Freedberg, *Iconoclasts and their motives*, Maarssen 1985

DE GELDER 1921
Jan Jacob de Gelder, *Bartolomeus van der Helst*, Rotterdam 1921

VAN GELDER 1937
H. E. van Gelder, *'s-Gravenhage in zeven eeuwen*, Amsterdam 1937

VAN GOGH
*The complete letters of Vincent van Gogh*, 3 vols., Greenwich, Conn. n.d.

HAAK 1984
B. Haak, *Hollandse schilders in de Gouden Eeuw*, Amsterdam 1984. Also published in English

HALEY 1972
K.H.D. Haley, *The Dutch in the seventeenth century*, London 1972

HAZEWINKEL 1975
H. C. Hazewinkel, *Geschiedenis van Rotterdam*, vol. 4, Zaltbommel 1975

HOUBRAKEN 1718-1721
Arnold Houbraken, *De groote schouburgh der Nederlantsche konstschilders en schilderessen*, 3 vols., Amsterdam 1718-1721

HUYGENS, BRIEFWISSELING
J. A. Worp, *De briefwisseling van Constantijn Huygens (1608-1687)*, 6 vols., The Hague 1911-1917

IMMERZEEL 1842-1843
J. Immerzeel Jr., *De levens en werken der Hollandsche en*

*Vlaamsche kunstschilders, beeldhouwers, graveurs en bouwmeesters*, 3 vols., Amsterdam 1842-1843

JACOBSEN JENSEN 1918
J.N. Jacobsen Jensen, 'Moryson's reis door en zijn karakteristiek van de Nederlanden,' *Bijdragen en Mededeelingen van het Historisch Genootschap* 39 (1918), pp.214-305

JANSON 1982
H.W. Janson, *Form follows function – or does it? Modernist design theory and the history of art*, The First Gerson Lecture, Maarssen 1982

DE JONGH 1973
E. de Jongh, ''tGotsche krulligh mall': de houding tegenover de gotiek in het zeventiende-eeuwse Holland,' *Nederlands Kunsthistorisch Jaarboek* 24 (1973), pp.85-145

DE JONGH 1986
E. de Jongh, *Portretten van echt en trouw: huwelijk en gezin in de Nederlandse kunst van de zeventiende eeuw*, Zwolle and Haarlem 1986

KOLB 1937
Marthe Kolb, *Ary Scheffer et son temps, 1795-1858*, Paris 1937

KRAMM 1857-1864
Christiaan Kramm, *De levens en werken der Hollandsche en Vlaamsche kunstschilders, beeldhouwers, graveurs en bouwmeesters, van den vroegsten tot op onzen tijd*, 4 vols., Amsterdam 1857-1864

KUIPER-RUEMPEL AND WOLLESWINKEL 1982
A. Kuiper-Ruempel and E. Wolleswinkel, *Bulletin van het Dordrechts Museum* 7:3-4 (July-August 1982)

DE LEEUW 1985
Ronald de Leeuw, 'Nederlandse Orientalisten,' *Jong Holland* 1 (1985), pp.10-37

LIEDTKE 1982
Walter A. Liedtke, *Architectural painting in Delft: Gerard Houckgeest, Hendrick van Vliet, Emanuel de Witte*, Doornspijk 1982

LUNSINGH SCHEURLEER 1962
Th.H. Lunsingh Scheurleer, 'Beeldhouwwerk in Huygens's Haagse huis,' *Oud-Holland* 77 (1962), pp.181-205

VAN LUTTERVELT 1947
R. van Luttervelt, 'Een zeegezicht met een historische voorstelling van Adam Willaerts,' *Historia* 12 (1947), pp.225-228

MACLAREN 1960
Neil MacLaren, *The Dutch School (National Gallery Catalogues)*, London 1960

MARTIN 1923-1924
W. Martin, 'Jan van Ravesteyn's *Magistraat en schutters, 1618,* en het ontwerp daarvoor,' *Oud-Holland* 41 (1923-1924), pp.193-198

MEIJER 1971
Th.J. Meijer, 'Brieven uit de studentenkerker,' *Leids Jaarboekje* 63 (1971), pp.43-64

MEISCHKE AND REESER 1983
R. Meischke and H.E. Reeser, eds., *Het Trippenhuis te Amsterdam*, Amsterdam etc. 1983

MIEDEMA 1981
Hessel Miedema, *Kunst, kunstenaar en kunstwerk bij Karel van Mander: een analyse van zijn levensbeschrijvingen*, Alphen aan den Rijn 1981

MONTIAS 1982
John Michael Montias, *Artists and artisans in Delft: a socio-economic study of the seventeenth century*, Princeton 1982

MULLER 1985
Sheila D. Muller, *Charity in the Dutch Republic: pictures of rich and poor for charitable institutions*, Ann Arbor, Michigan 1985 (revision of a Ph.D. thesis for the University of California, Berkeley)

NIEMEIJER 1968
J.W. Niemeijer, exhib. cat. *Egbert van Drielst, 'De Drentse Hobbema,' 1745-1818*, Assen (Provinciaal Museum van Drenthe) 1968

NNBW
*Nieuw Nederlands Biografisch Woordenboek*, 10 vols., Leiden 1911-1937

PELINCK 1953
E. Pelinck, 'Paulus van Spijk en zijn verzameling,' *Leids Jaarboekje* 45 (1953), pp.120-123

PELINCK 1956
E. Pelinck, 'De vergaderzaal van Kunst Wordt door Arbeid Verkregen,' *Leids Jaarboekje* 48 (1956), pp.154-160

PIPPEL 1941
J.G. Pippel, *In en om de hofstad: Den Haag in den loop der tijden en hoe onze voorouders er leefden*, 's-Gravenhage 1941

RAUWS 1936-37
H. Rauws, 'Gerard Pietersz. Hulft,' *Historia* 2 (1936-1937), p. 260ff

ROSENBERG, SLIVE AND TER KUILE 1966
Jakob Rosenberg, Seymour Slive and E.H. ter Kuile, *Dutch art and architecture, 1600 to 1800*, Harmondsworth etc. 1966

SCHAMA 1977
Simon Schama, *Patriots and liberators: revolution in the Netherlands, 1780-1813*, New York 1977

SCHATBORN 1985
P. Schatborn, exhib. cat. *Drawings by Rembrandt, his anonymous pupil and followers* (Catalogue of the Dutch and Flemish drawings in the Rijksprentenkabinet, Amsterdam, vol. 4), The Hague 1985

VAN SCHENDEL 1975
Elie van Schendel, cat. *Museum Mesdag: Nederlandse negentiende-eeuwse schilderijen, tekeningen en grafiek*, The Hague 1975

SCHOTEL 1853
G.D.J. Schotel, *Anna Maria van Schuurman*, 's-Hertogenbosch 1853

SCHWARTZ 1966-1967
Gary Schwartz, 'Saenredam, Huygens and the Utrecht bull,' *Simiolus: Kunsthistorisch Tijdschrift* 1 (1966-1967), pp. 69-93

SCHWARTZ 1983
Gary Schwartz, 'Jan van der Heyden and the Huydecopers of Maarsseveen,' *J. Paul Getty Museum Journal* 11 (1983), pp. 197-220

SCHWARTZ 1985
Gary Schwartz, *Rembrandt, his life, his paintings: a new biography with all accessible paintings illustrated in colour*, Harmondsworth etc. 1985

SLIVE 1974
Seymour Slive, *Frans Hals*, vol. 3, *Catalogue*, London 1974

STARING 1953
A. S(taring)., 'Een Leidsch verzamelaar en zijn lijfschilder,' *Leids Jaarboekje* 45 (1953), pp. 114-119

STONE-FERRIER 1985
Linda A. Stone-Ferrier, *Images of textiles: the weave of seventeenth-century Dutch art and society*, Ann Arbor, Michigan 1985 (revision of a Ph.D. thesis for the University of California, Berkeley)

TAVERNE 1972-1973
E. Taverne, 'Salomon de Bray and the reorganization of the Haarlem Guild of St. Luke in 1631,' *Simiolus* 6 (1972-1973), pp. 50-66

TEMPLE 1693
Sir William Temple, *Observations upon the United Provinces of the Netherlands*, 6th ed., London 1693

TENGNAGEL 1969
Mattheus Gansneb Tengnagel, *Alle werken*, ed. J.J. Oversteegen, Amsterdam 1969

VAN THIEL 1968
P.J.J. van Thiel, 'De kerk te Sloten door Jan Abrahamsz. Beerstraten,' *Bulletin van het Rijksmuseum* 16 (1968), pp. 51-56

VAN THIEL 1983
P.J.J. van Thiel, 'Werner van den Valckert,' *Oud-Holland* 97 (1983), pp. 128-195

VEENHOVEN 1969
A. Veenhoven, *Historie van Coevorden*, Groningen 1969

VOS 1653
Jan Vos, 'Strydt tusschen de Doodt en Natuur, of zeege der Schilderkunst' (Struggle between Death and Nature, or The Triumph of Painting), first published in September 1653 as a separate booklet, then once more in the more readily accessible anthology *Klioos kraam*, vol. 1, Leeuwarden 1656, pp. 16-31

WHITE 1982
Christopher White, *The Dutch paintings in the collection of Her Majesty the Queen*, Cambridge (England) 1982

WIJNMAN 1959
H. Wijnman, 'De schilder Abraham van den Tempel,' in *Uit de kring van Rembrandt en Vondel: verzamelde studies over hun leven en omgeving*, Amsterdam 1959, pp. 39-93

WORP
See Huygens, *Briefwisseling*

WURZBACH 1906-1911
Alfred von Wurzbach, *Niederländisches Künstler-Lexikon, auf Grund archivalischer Forschungen bearbeitet*, 3 vols., Vienna 1906-1911, reprint Amsterdam 1968

# Lenders to the exhibition

AMSTERDAM, AMSTERDAMS HISTORISCH MUSEUM
Cat.nrs.13, 15, 16, 34, 36, 69, 75 (unavailable for the exhibition), 77

AMSTERDAM, RIJKSMUSEUM
Cat.nrs.2, 3, 14, 22, 25, 33, 40, 52, 54, 55, 74, 76; fig.3

AMSTERDAM, RIJKSMUSEUM VINCENT VAN GOGH (VINCENT VAN GOGH FOUNDATION)
Fig.9

AMSTERDAM, STEDELIJK MUSEUM
Cat.nr.9

ARNHEM, GEMEENTEMUSEUM
Cat.nr.7

DELFT, MUSEUM HET PRINSENHOF
Cat.nr.81

DORDRECHT, DORDRECHTS MUSEUM
Cat.nr.56

ENSCHEDE, RIJKSMUSEUM TWENTHE
Cat.nr.18

FRANEKER, MUSEUM 'T COOPMANSHÛS
Cat.nrs.57, 58, 59, 60, 61, 62, 65, 68

HAARLEM, FRANS HALSMUSEUM
Cat.nrs.11, 29, 30

THE HAGUE, GEMEENTEMUSEUM
Cat.nrs.37, 83, 84, 85, 89, 90, 93; figs.6, 8

THE HAGUE, MAURITSHUIS
Cat.nr.19; fig.1

THE HAGUE, RIJKSMUSEUM H.W. MESDAG
Cat.nrs.8, 26

THE HAGUE AND AMSTERDAM, THE NETHERLANDS OFFICE FOR FINE ARTS (Rijksdienst Beeldende Kunst)

Cat.nrs.12, 17, 20, 23, 24, 27, 38, 39, 41, 53, 78, 79, 82, 86, 87, 88, 94, 95, 96, 97

LEEUWARDEN, FRIES MUSEUM
Cat.nrs.6, 10, 42-51, 91, 92

LEIDEN, MUSEUM BOERHAAVE
Cat.nrs.70-73

LEIDEN, STEDELIJK MUSEUM DE LAKENHAL
Cat.nrs.1, 4, 5, 32, 80

LEIDEN, RIJKSUNIVERSITEIT
Cat.nrs.63, 64, 66

ROTTERDAM, MUSEUM BOYMANS-VAN BEUNINGEN
Cat.nrs.31, 35

UTRECHT, RIJKSMUSEUM HET CATHARIJNECONVENT
Cat.nr.21

UTRECHT, CENTRAAL MUSEUM
Cat.nr.28; not in catalogue: Jan van Scorel (copy after), *Pope Adrian VI*

UTRECHT, UNIVERSITEITSMUSEUM
Cat.nr.67

The insurance for the exhibition has been provided by the Government of Canada through the Insurance Program for Travelling Exhibitions, administrated by the Department of Commerce under Minister Marcel Masse.

Photographs and colour transparencies were kindly made available by the lenders.

# Index of artists

The italic numerals refer to figure numbers.

## HOLLAND
### HEART OF THE ARTS

KLM Royal Dutch Airlines, founded in 1919, is the world's oldest airline still operating under its own name.

Today KLM is the world's sixth largest with a network spanning 128 destinations in 78 countries around the world. During KLM's long history the airline has maintained a commitment to quality service, it has been innovative and has remained financially sound.

In recognition of this, KLM was in 1985 selected 'Airline of the Year' by the prestigious aviation journal *Air Transport World*. This award is an exceptional honour for the national carrier of one of the world's smallest countries... the Netherlands.

Every year over 5 million passengers and 300,000 tons of cargo are carried by KLM around the world.

### KLM – cargo specialists
At KLM cargo has always played an important role, since the first flight from London to Amsterdam, which carried KLM's first cargo shipment... a bundle of newspapers. During the years KLM has gathered a tremendous amount of knowhow in transporting a diversity of goods such as perishables, livestock as well as art shipments. A major art work that KLM carried recently from New York to Amsterdam's Stedelijk Museum of Art was Fernand Léger's *La Grande Parade*.

### KLM to Vancouver
On April 1, 1986, KLM, the world's oldest airline, became Vancouver's newest as scheduled service from Amsterdam began. To mark this occasion and to honour Vancouver's Centennial KLM has sponsored this unique *Dutch world of painting* exhibition.

## KLM

KLM Royal Dutch Airlines
Reliable – Punctual – Careful – Friendly